Simply Vegan Baking

TAKING THE FUSS OUT OF VEGAN CAKES, COOKIES, BREADS AND DESSERTS

FREYA COX

Photography by Clare Winfield

HARPER DESIGN

An Imprint of HarperCollins Publishers

Published in 2022 by
Harper Design
An Imprint of HarperCollins*Publishers*
195 Broadway
New York, NY 10007
Tel: (212) 207-7000
Fax: (855) 746-6023
harperdesign@harpercollins.com
www.hc.com

Distributed throughout the world by
HarperCollins Publishers
195 Broadway
New York, NY 10007

For Murdoch Books, an imprint of Allen & Unwin:
Publisher: Céline Hughes
Art Direction and Design: Nikki Ellis
Photographer: Clare Winfield
Food Stylists: Freya Cox and Joanna Jackson
Prop Stylist: Hannah Wilkinson
Production Director, UK: Niccolò De Bianchi
Production Director, Australia: Lou Playfair

ISBN 978-0-06-3272613
Printed in China
First Printing, 2022

OVEN GUIDE: You may find cooking times vary depending on the oven you are using. The recipes in this book are based on fan-assisted oven temperatures. For non-fan-assisted ovens, as a general rule, set the oven temperature to 20°C (35°F) higher than indicated in the recipe.

INTRODUCTION

I have always been a very passionate person, so when I first got into vegan baking, I automatically fell in love with it. I am a massive foodie: it's something that not only brings me joy personally but allows others to come together and enjoy one another's company. The way a loved one's face lights up when they are given something homemade is a feeling I will never tire of. I initially learned to bake with my gran when I was young. I would leave her house on a Sunday with boxes full of cakes, devastated the weekend was over. We would bake gifts for birthdays, Christmas and pretty much every occasion. That's where I fell in love with it.

I went pretty much head first into the vegan diet once I made the connection between animals and food and I struggled to look back. My dad has been vegan for around seven years and has played a huge part in helping me with the transition. He has always been an inspiring person; I owe him a lot for encouraging me in the right direction. It's fair to say I couldn't have written this book without him. My mum has always pushed me to do what I love; I feel incredibly lucky to have had her support from day one. I'm a bit of a perfectionist so creating recipes isn't always smooth sailing. I also have Maggie, a fellow GBBO contestant and now close friend, to thank for testing lots of my recipes.

I am very understanding that it isn't possible for everyone to make the change to eating completely vegan straight away. Veganism is a big lifestyle change, and not something I believe should be forced upon each and every one of us. Small changes also have a big impact and help move towards a more sustainable view of veganism as a whole. We need to build a society where making an effort is praised. In turn this makes veganism less daunting to those who may be interested in making the change. Throughout this book I have included key tips and tricks that I have found helpful throughout my transition to vegan baking, with the hope of making it a little easier for others. The recipes throughout vary from simple bakes like fruit crumble slices and chocolate fudge cupcakes for those who are looking for a recipe that is completely faff free, to more elaborate celebration cakes to impress any crowd. A key thing I wanted to be sure of when writing these recipes was that all the ingredients are accessible in large supermarkets. I still feel there is an assumption

that vegan baking requires unusual ingredients that are difficult to find, however it doesn't need to be this way. Simple swaps like soya milk instead of whole milk and vegan baking block instead of butter work perfectly. In the little tips section before each chapter, I talk about these swaps in more detail.

I feel there is something special about creating a recipe that has all the flavours and textures of traditional, well-loved bakes while knowing that no animal products are involved. I love every single one of the recipes inside this book, and both my vegan and non-vegan friends agree there is no sacrifice in quality: I'd argue they are 'unbelievably vegan'. One of the biggest struggles people face when getting into vegan baking is knowing where to start – it can seem daunting at first. Hopefully this book will ease this feeling and inspire others to make whatever change they can. Whether you use the recipes as part of a vegan lifestyle, as a way to eat more plant-based food, or just because the recipes are delicious, I hope you try these recipes and enjoy them as much as I do.

Try your best to follow the recipes as closely as you can but make the most of your time baking and don't take things too seriously! I always tell people who are getting into baking not to stress themselves out; at the end of the day it is just cake. It will near enough always taste amazing even if it doesn't come out perfectly every time – though I am certain your bakes will all come out perfectly.

Lots of love,

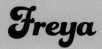

Cakes

A very common question I get asked is: "what do you use instead of eggs?" I have never been a fan of chia or flax eggs in cakes – I don't feel they give the same fluffy moist texture. I use a plant milk and acidic liquid mixture for my cake recipes and this replaces the eggs. It is very important for standard cake recipes that you use soya milk; I use sweetened, but non-sweetened also works great. The protein content in soya milk is much higher than in almond or oat, for example, which produces a much fluffier cake that rises well. For the acidic element I use apple cider vinegar, however if you don't have this, lemon juice also works great. Once added to the soya milk it curdles, creating a cake that is for sure 'unbelievably vegan'. Lastly, I recommend that you warm the soya milk through before adding the vinegar. This just helps it to curdle, creating the perfect cake every time.

VICTORIA SPONGE CAKE

Bake it Simple You could also fill the cake with a layer of American buttercream (see page 171) for a slightly sweeter cake.

The absolute classic of all cake recipes, but it can still be one of the hardest things to get right. This simple-to-follow recipe ensures you make the perfect Victoria sponge every time.

1. Preheat the oven to 180°C (350°F) fan. Grease two 15cm (6 inch) cake tins with butter and line with baking parchment.

2. Put the soya milk in a jug and heat in the microwave for 1 minute to warm through (alternatively you can do this in a pan on the hob). Once warmed, mix in the apple cider vinegar and place to the side to curdle – this will take about 5 minutes.

3. Meanwhile, sift the flour, sugar, bicarbonate of soda and salt into a large bowl. Make a well in the middle of the dry ingredients.

4. Once the soya milk has curdled, add the vegetable oil and the vanilla extract to the same jug and mix. Add the wet ingredients to the dry and combine using a balloon whisk until just combined – try not to over-whisk.

5. Divide the batter between the cake tins and bake for 25–30 minutes, or until a skewer inserted into the cakes comes out clean. Leave the tins on a cooling rack until cool enough to touch before removing the cakes from the tins to cool completely.

6. Once cool, peel off the parchment from the bottom of the cakes. If the cakes are slightly domed on the top, level one of them by cutting off the top with a sharp knife to make it easier to stack the second.

7. Spread the raspberry jam evenly over the levelled cake, then place the second cake on top. Sprinkle the 1 tablespoon of sugar over the top to serve. Enjoy!

For the sponge:
vegan butter, for greasing

225ml (7¾fl oz) soya milk

1 tbsp apple cider vinegar

235g (8½oz) plain (all-purpose) flour

210g (7½oz) caster (granulated) sugar, plus 1 tbsp to sprinkle on top

1 tsp bicarbonate of soda (baking soda)

½ tsp salt

90ml (3fl oz) vegetable oil

1 tbsp vanilla extract

For the filling:
150g (5½oz) raspberry jam (see page 169, or use shop-bought if preferred)

Serves 8–10

BLACK FOREST GATEAU

I love every recipe in this book, but this chocolate cake has to be my favourite. I spent so long trying so many different methods as I just never found a chocolate cake I really loved. This is so moist and has a rich chocolate flavour. It is the perfect cake to take to any celebration – a real showstopper!

1. Preheat the oven to 180°C (350°F) fan. Grease three 20cm (8 inch) cake tins with butter and line with baking parchment.

2. Put the soya milk in a jug and heat in the microwave for 1 minute to warm through (alternatively you can do this in a pan on the hob). Once warmed, mix in the apple cider vinegar and place to the side to curdle – this will take about 5 minutes.

3. Meanwhile, sift the flour, sugar, bicarbonate of soda, cocoa powder, espresso powder and salt into a large bowl. Make a well in the middle of the dry ingredients.

4. Once the soya milk has curdled, add the vegetable oil and the vanilla to the same jug and mix. Add the wet mixture to the dry ingredients and combine using a balloon whisk until just combined and you have a smooth glossy batter – try not to over-whisk.

5. Divide the batter between the cake tins. Bake for 25 minutes, or until a skewer inserted into the centre of the cakes comes out clean. Leave the tins on a cooling rack until cool enough to touch before removing the cakes from the tins to cool completely.

6. Meanwhile, make the American buttercream using the quantities listed opposite and following the directions on page 171, adding in the kirsch instead of the plant milk and vanilla. Place half of the buttercream into a piping bag fitted with a round nozzle.

7. Once the cakes are completely cool, choose the flattest one and set aside to use for the top. Place a cake onto your serving plate or cake board and pipe blobs of buttercream around the edge of the cake. Place a spoonful of buttercream in the middle of the cake and spread out with a spatula being careful not to damage your piped edge.

8. Spoon one-third of the jam onto the buttercream in the centre of the cake and spread evenly, don't worry if some jam runs to the side, I think it looks even better this way. Place the next cake on top and repeat the fillings, then place the top cake and repeat, decorating this layer with the fresh cherries to finish. Enjoy!

For the chocolate cake:
vegan butter, for greasing

340ml (12fl oz) soya milk

1½ tbsp apple cider vinegar

290g (10¼oz) plain (all-purpose) flour

315g (11oz) caster (granulated) sugar

1½ tsp bicarbonate of soda (baking soda)

60g (2oz) cocoa powder

1½ tbsp espresso powder (must be powder not granules)

¾ tsp salt

130ml (4¼fl oz) vegetable oil

1 tbsp vanilla extract

For the kirsch American buttercream:
250g (9oz) vegan butter block

500g (1lb 2oz) icing (confectioners') sugar

2 tbsp kirsch (optional)

250g (9oz) cherry jam (see page 168, or use shop-bought jam if preferred)

a handful of fresh cherries

Serves 12–16

CARROT CAKE

Carrot cake is my brother's favourite, with mountains of smooth cream cheese frosting, of course. I like to add in dried cranberries for little sour bursts throughout – they work perfectly with the crunch of walnut pieces.

1. Preheat the oven to 180°C (350°F) fan. Grease two 15cm (6 inch) cake tins with butter and line with baking parchment.

2. Put the soya milk in a jug and heat in the microwave for 1 minute to warm through (alternatively you can do this in a pan on the hob). Once warmed, mix in the apple cider vinegar and place to the side to curdle – this will take about 5 minutes.

3. Put the flour, sugar, bicarbonate of soda, baking powder, salt, orange zest and spices in a large mixing bowl and whisk together until fully combined.

4. Once the soya milk has curdled, add the oil to the same jug and mix. Pour the wet ingredients into the dry ingredients and whisk together until a smooth, lump-free batter forms, then stir in the grated carrot, chopped walnuts and cranberries until evenly distributed.

5. Divide the mixture between the two cake tins and bake for 40–45 minutes or until a skewer inserted into the centre of the cakes comes out clean. Leave the tins on a cooling rack until cool enough to touch before removing the cakes from the tins to cool completely.

6. Meanwhile, make the cream cheese frosting. Beat the butter and icing sugar together until light and creamy (use a stand mixer if you have one). Add the cream cheese and beat until fully combined and you have a smooth creamy frosting. Spoon half of the cream cheese frosting into a piping bag fitted with a star nozzle.

7. Choose the flattest of the two cakes to be the top cake. Spread some of the frosting from the bowl over the top of both cakes and use an angled palette knife or the back of a spoon to create a swirl on the cake you have chosen to go on top. Pipe the rest of the frosting around the outside edge of the two cakes, then stack the two together. Finish off the cake with a sprinkle of extra walnuts and dried cranberries. Enjoy!

For the sponge:

vegan butter, for greasing

225ml (7¾fl oz) soya milk

1 tbsp apple cider vinegar

235g (8½oz) self-raising flour

210g (7½oz) soft light brown sugar

½ tsp bicarbonate of soda (baking soda)

½ tsp baking powder

½ tsp salt

zest of 1 orange

1½ tsp ground cinnamon

½ tsp ground nutmeg

½ tsp ground ginger

90ml (3fl oz) vegetable oil

150g (5½oz) grated carrot

50g (1¾oz) chopped walnuts (or any nut of choice), plus extra for topping

70g (2½oz) dried cranberries (or any dried fruit of choice), plus extra for topping

For the cream cheese frosting:

100g (3½oz) vegan butter

460g (1lb) icing (confectioners') sugar

170g (6oz) vegan cream cheese

Serves 8–10

COFFEE AND WALNUT CAKE

Bake it Simple The great thing about blitzing the praline into a crumb is that it doesn't matter if your sugar crystallizes – it works just as well!

Russian buttercream is much silkier and slightly less sweet than traditional American buttercream, making it the perfect accompaniment to the crunchy walnut praline. A modern twist on a true classic.

1. Preheat the oven to 180°C (350°F) fan. Grease two 15cm (6 inch) cake tins with butter and line with baking parchment.

2. Put the soya milk in a jug and heat in the microwave for 1 minute to warm through (alternatively you can do this in a pan on the hob). Once warmed, mix in the apple cider vinegar and place to the side to curdle – this will take about 5 minutes.

3. Meanwhile sift the flour, sugar, bicarbonate of soda, coffee powder and salt into a large bowl. Make a well in the middle of the dry ingredients.

4. Once the soya milk has curdled, add the vegetable oil and the vanilla extract to the same jug and mix. Add the wet mixture to the dry ingredients and combine using a balloon whisk until just combined – try not to over-whisk.

5. Divide the batter evenly between the cake tins. Bake for 25 minutes, or until a skewer inserted into the centre of the cakes comes out clean. Leave on a cooling rack in the tins until cool enough to touch before removing the cakes from the tins to cool completely.

6. For the Russian buttercream, put the butter in the bowl of a stand mixer if you have one – or into a large mixing bowl if you are using an electric hand whisk – and mix on high speed until it is very pale in colour and fluffy. You don't want to rush this step – mix it for at least 10 minutes. Once the butter is light and fluffy, slowly add the condensed milk, 2 tablespoons at a time, allowing it to combine fully between each addition.

7. Once all of the condensed milk has been added, add the coffee powder – I add 4 tablespoons as I like it strong. Finally, add the icing sugar, beating until a smooth shiny buttercream is formed. Place in the fridge whilst you make the praline.

8. For the walnut praline, cover a baking tray with a sheet of baking parchment and place to the side.

9. Put the sugar in a saucepan with 55ml (1¾fl oz) water and set over a low–medium heat, swirling the pan occasionally until the sugar starts to dissolve and the liquid becomes clear. Once clear, turn the heat up to medium and leave, without stirring, until it starts to turn a golden amber colour. The edges will turn first so at this point you can swirl the pan a little, so it colours evenly.

10. Once the caramel is an amber colour, take the pan off the heat and quickly add the butter and the chopped walnuts. Stir until the nuts are evenly coated in caramel, then pour onto the lined baking tray and spread out, then leave to cool. Once cool, break the praline into shards and place in a food processor. Blitz the praline to a crumb, leaving a few slightly larger chunks. If you don't have a food processor, place the praline in a sandwich bag and use a rolling pin to bash the praline to crumbs.

11. To assemble, level the top of one of the sponges with a sharp knife – this will be the base sponge. Spread an even layer of the coffee buttercream over the base sponge (or you can pipe it on if you prefer). Sprinkle over a generous layer of praline crumbs, then place the second sponge on top. Cover the top of the cake with a thick layer of the buttercream, using a palate knife to spread it out and create a little swirl effect, if you wish.

12. Use the rest of the buttercream to roughly cover the sides of the cake, then coat them with the remaining praline – just use your hands to press it into the buttercream. Enjoy!

For the sponge:
vegan butter, for greasing

225ml (7¾fl oz) soya milk

1 tbsp apple cider vinegar

235g (8½oz) plain (all-purpose) flour

210g (7½oz) caster (granulated) sugar

1 tsp bicarbonate of soda (baking soda)

3 tbsp instant coffee powder (if you don't have powder, dissolve the same amount of granules in a small amount of water)

½ tsp salt

90ml (3fl oz) vegetable oil

2 tsp vanilla extract

For the Russian buttercream:
250g (9oz) vegan butter (Flora Plant works well for this)

1 x 370g (13oz) can of vegan condensed milk

3–4 tbsp instant coffee powder

50g (1¾oz) icing (confectioners') sugar

For the walnut praline:
225g (8oz) granulated sugar

7g (¼oz) vegan butter

100g (3½oz) walnuts, broken into pieces

Serves 8–10

GLUTEN-FREE LEMON AND PASSION FRUIT CAKE WITH RUM DRIZZLE

This is a proper celebration cake. It has four layers of sponge filled with silky smooth Swiss meringue buttercream and a tangy passion fruit curd. I sometimes find gluten-free cakes to have a funny texture, but the rum drizzle helps the sponge retain moisture. This is the perfect birthday cake for someone special.

1. Preheat the oven to 180°C (350°F) fan. Grease four 20cm (8 inch) cake tins with butter and line with baking parchment.

2. Put the soya milk in a jug and heat in the microwave for 1 minute to warm through (alternatively you can do this in a pan on the hob). Once warmed, mix in the apple cider vinegar and place to the side to curdle – this will take about 5 minutes.

3. Meanwhile, sift the flour, sugar, bicarbonate of soda, xanthan gum and salt into a large bowl. Add the lemon zest and make a well in the middle of the dry ingredients.

4. Once the soya milk has curdled, add the vegetable oil and the vanilla extract to the same jug and mix. Add the wet mixture to the dry ingredients and combine using a balloon whisk until just combined – try not to over-whisk.

5. Divide the batter between the cake tins and bake for 25–30 minutes, or until a skewer inserted into the centre of the cakes comes out clean. Leave on a cooling rack in the tins until cool enough to touch before removing the cakes from the tins.

6. Whilst the cakes are cooling, make the rum syrup. Put the lemon juice, sugar and rum in a saucepan over a medium heat and stir until the sugar is fully dissolved, then leave to cool slightly.

7. Whilst they are still cooling, use a skewer to prick the cakes, then drizzle spoonfuls of the syrup over the surface of the cakes. Don't over-soak the cakes – just add a light drizzle of syrup. There will be syrup left that can be used for the buttercream later. Leave the cakes to cool completely.

Continued overleaf...

For the sponge:
vegan butter, for greasing

450ml (16fl oz) soya milk

2 tbsp apple cider vinegar

470g (1lb ½oz) gluten-free self-raising flour (I use Doves Farm)

420g (15oz) caster (granulated) sugar

1½ tsp bicarbonate of soda (baking soda)

1 tsp xanthan gum

1 tsp salt

zest of 4 lemons

175ml (5½fl oz) vegetable oil (or any neutral oil)

1 tbsp vanilla extract

For the lemon and rum drizzle:
juice of 6 lemons

50g (1¾oz) granulated sugar

3 tbsp white rum

For the filling:
1 recipe quantity of Swiss meringue buttercream (see page 172)

1 jar of passion fruit curd (see page 170)

For the flower decorations:
½ recipe quantity of American buttercream (see page 171)

food colours such as pink, purple, yellow and green

Serves 12–16

8. Add 1 tablespoon of the remaining lemon and rum drizzle (that you didn't pour over the sponges) to the Swiss meringue buttercream to flavour it. Place one-quarter of the buttercream into a piping bag fitted with a round nozzle.

9. To assemble, place a cake on the serving platter or cake board, then pipe a line of buttercream around the edge of the cake to stop any curd spilling out. Spoon one-third of the curd into the centre of the cake and spread evenly. Dollop a spoonful of the buttercream on top of the curd and spread out in an even layer, then place the next cake on top.

10. Repeat the above step with the remaining cakes until it is fully stacked. Once stacked, crumb coat the cake – meaning you cover the sides and top with a thin but smooth layer. You can use an angled spatula or a scraper to make it as smooth as possible. Place the cake in the fridge to firm up for 10 minutes.

11. Take the chilled cake out of the fridge and use the remaining buttercream to cover the cake, smoothing the sides and top with a scraper if you have one. (You can add colour to this buttercream before coating the cake if you wish – I used a mint green.)

12. If decorating with flowers, divide the American buttercream between multiple bowls and colour with your desired colours. Pipe your flowers and leave them in the freezer to firm up before placing onto the cake. If you don't want to pipe flowers, you can just pipe directly onto the cake to decorate however you fancy! Enjoy!

CHOCOLATE CHIP BANANA BREAD

Bake it Simple If you like spices, try adding in a teaspoon of ground cinnamon and ginger.

I shamelessly admit that I made banana bread every week during lockdown. I genuinely love it, particularly when it's filled with chocolate chips and toasted until the edges are crisp.

1. Preheat the oven to 180°C (350°F) fan. Grease a loaf tin with butter and line with baking parchment, or use a loaf tin liner.

2. Put the bananas in a large mixing bowl and mash thoroughly – I use a potato masher, but a fork will also work. Add the oil and soft brown sugar and mix with a wooden spoon until fully combined. Add the flour and baking powder and mix until fully incorporated. Finally, add the chopped walnuts and chocolate and fold in until evenly distributed.

3. Transfer the batter to the lined cake tin and bake for 1 hour, covering with foil after 30 minutes to stop the top from browning too much. Once baked, place on a cooling rack to cool for a few minutes, then remove from the tin to cool completely. Enjoy!

vegan butter, for greasing

3 large overripe bananas, peeled

75ml (2½fl oz) vegetable oil, or any neutral oil

100g (3½oz) soft light brown sugar

225g (8oz) plain (all-purpose) flour

2 tsp baking powder

50g (1¾oz) chopped walnuts

100g (3½oz) vegan chocolate chips

Makes 1 loaf (10–12 slices)

CHOCOLATE ORANGE BATTENBERG

I personally think Battenberg is a very underrated cake. Chocolate orange is, in my opinion, an upgraded version of a traditional Battenberg, but the marzipan covering is a necessity whatever flavour you make.

1. Preheat the oven to 180°C (350°F) fan. If you have a 20 x 25cm (8 x 10 inch) Battenberg tin, grease it with butter and line with baking parchment. If not, use a brownie tin of the same size and cut a piece of cardboard the same length as the long side of the tin. Stick the cardboard down to the centre of the tin with sticky tape, then grease and line each side with baking parchment — I don't have a Battenberg tin and this works great for me!

2. Put the soya milk in a jug and heat in the microwave for 1 minute to warm through (alternatively you can do this in a pan on the hob). Once warmed, mix in the apple cider vinegar and place to the side to curdle — this will take about 5 minutes.

3. Meanwhile, sift the flour, sugar, bicarbonate of soda and salt into a large bowl. Make a well in the middle of the dry ingredients.

4. Once the soya milk has curdled, add the vegetable oil and the vanilla extract to the same jug and mix. Add the wet mixture to the dry ingredients and combine using a balloon whisk until just combined — try not to over-whisk.

5. Divide the batter between two bowls, then add the extra 20g (¾oz) of flour and orange zest into one bowl and stir to combine fully. Add the orange food colouring and mix in, then pour this into one side of the Battenberg or brownie tin.

6. Add the cocoa powder to the other bowl and mix fully, then pour the chocolate batter into the other side of the tin.

7. Bake for 25–30 minutes, or until a skewer inserted into the centre of the cake comes out clean. Leave on a cooling rack in the tin until cool enough to touch before carefully removing the cakes from the tin to cool completely.

Continued overleaf...

For the sponge:
vegan butter, for greasing

225ml (7¾fl oz) soya milk

1 tbsp apple cider vinegar

195g (7oz) plain (all-purpose) flour, plus an extra 20g (¾oz) for the orange cake

210g (7½oz) caster (granulated) sugar

1 tsp bicarbonate of soda (baking soda)

½ tsp salt

90ml (3fl oz) vegetable oil

1 tbsp vanilla extract

zest of 1 orange

orange food colouring (optional)

20g (¾oz) cocoa powder

For the orange American buttercream:
125g (4½oz) vegan butter

250g (9oz) icing (confectioners') sugar

juice of ½ orange (or to taste)

For filling and coating:
450g (1lb) marzipan (shop-bought blocks are generally vegan)

50g (1¾oz) apricot jam

Serves 10–12

Bake it Simple If you aren't the biggest buttercream fan, try sandwiching the cakes with marmalade for extra orange flavour.

8. Make the orange American buttercream using the quantities listed on page 28 and following the directions on page 171, adding in the orange juice instead of the plant milk and vanilla.

9. Dust a work surface with icing sugar and roll out the marzipan to a rectangle that is large enough to cover the whole cake – at least 30 x 35cm (12 x 14 inches).

10. Once the cakes are cool, trim the dome off each if they have risen slightly, then cut each side in half so you have four long strips of cake. Cover the long edge of one orange cake with a good layer of buttercream, then stick a chocolate cake to it, so it is sitting next to it. Cover the top of these two quarters with a good layer of buttercream.

11. Repeat the previous step to sandwich the remaining cakes, then place these on top, flipping the colours so that the orange sits on top of the chocolate cake and vice versa, forming a checkerboard effect. Place the cake in the fridge for 15 minutes so the buttercream can firm up.

12. If the apricot jam is too thick to spread, put it in the microwave for a few seconds to melt slightly, then spread it across the surface of the marzipan. Place the cake widthways in the centre of the marzipan – the short side of the marzipan should be around the same length as the cake. Fold the marzipan up and over the sides of the cake to cover, trimming any excess where the two sides join at the top. Flip the cake over so the seam side is facing down.

13. If you have any leftover marzipan, you can roll it into little balls for decoration on top of the cake. You can also use a blowtorch to slightly caramelize the top, if you like. When you are ready to serve, trim both ends of the cake to reveal a perfect Battenberg. Enjoy!

CHOCOLATE YULE LOG

This Yule log is a necessity at Christmas time. The filling uses a whipped white chocolate ganache that balances the slightly bitter dark chocolate covering. The white swirl inside the log is sure to leave guests impressed.

1. Preheat the oven to 180°C (350°F) fan. Grease a 33 x 25cm (13 x 10 inch) baking tray with butter and line with baking parchment.

2. Put the aquafaba and cream of tartar into the bowl of a stand mixer, if you have one – or into a large mixing bowl if you are using an electric hand whisk – and mix on medium–high speed until stiff peaks are formed. This means the aquafaba doesn't move, even when tipped upside down.

3. Meanwhile, put the milk in a jug and heat in the microwave for 1 minute to warm through (alternatively you can do this in a pan on the hob). Once warmed, mix in the apple cider vinegar and place to the side to curdle – this will take about 5 minutes.

4. Put the flour, sugar, cocoa powder, salt, baking powder and bicarbonate of soda in a large mixing bowl. Mix with a balloon whisk until fully combined.

5. Add the oil and the curdled milk to the dry ingredients and mix until fully combined. The mixture will be very stiff and dry at this point, but that's normal.

6. Gently fold the aquafaba into the mixture, one spoonful at a time, trying not to knock out too much air. It will become a much looser mixture as you add more aquafaba.

7. Pour the mixture into the lined baking tray and level out the top until smooth. Bake for 12–15 minutes until a skewer comes out clean.

8. Whilst the sponge is baking, lay out a piece of baking parchment the size of the sponge and cover it with a generous sprinkle of caster sugar.

For the sponge:
vegan butter, for greasing

150g (5½oz) aquafaba (see page 149)

¼ tsp cream of tartar

90ml (3fl oz) soya milk

1 tbsp apple cider vinegar

160g (5¾oz) plain (all-purpose) flour

190g (6¾oz) caster (granulated) sugar, plus extra for rolling

40g (1½oz) cocoa powder

½ tsp salt

½ tsp baking powder

¼ tsp bicarbonate of soda (baking soda)

75ml (2½fl oz) vegetable oil

For the filling:
150ml (5fl oz) vegan double (heavy) cream

200g (7oz) vegan white chocolate, broken into pieces

40g (1½oz) vegan butter, melted

For the coating:
1 recipe quantity of Chocolate Ganache (see page 171)

icing (confectioners') sugar, for dusting

Serves 10

Continued overleaf...

9. Once the sponge is baked, let it stand for a minute or so until the tin is cool enough to touch, then tip the sponge out, top-side-down, onto the sugar-covered parchment. Gently remove the baking parchment from the bottom of the sponge, then cover with a damp tea towel and leave to cool (this stops the sponge from drying out).

10. To make the filling, heat the cream either in a bowl in the microwave or in a saucepan on the hob until gently boiling, then take off the heat. Add the white chocolate to the hot cream, making sure it is all covered by the cream, and leave to stand for a minute before stirring to a smooth lump-free ganache. Add the melted butter and mix until fully combined, then leave to cool completely – I tend to place it in the freezer for half an hour or so. It will thicken up as it cools.

11. Once the white chocolate filling is completely cold, transfer it to the bowl of a stand mixer, if you have one, or alternatively to a large mixing bowl. Whisk until the ganache becomes light and fluffy, but don't over-whisk or it will become difficult to spread.

12. Once the sponge is cool, use a sharp knife to make an incision line widthways across the sponge, 2.5cm (1 inch) in from one of the short sides, cutting only halfway into the sponge and not all the way through (this just makes it easier to roll).

13. Spread the filling out across the sponge, then carefully but confidently roll it up from the short side where you made the incision. Use the baking parchment to help you roll the sponge. Don't panic if the sponge cracks slightly – it will be covered in ganache.

14. Make the dark chocolate ganache (see page 171), and once it is cool and becomes spreadable, cover the Yule log with it. Once the ganache has set, lightly dust the Yule log with icing sugar. Enjoy!

RASPBERRY SWISS ROLL

Bake it Simple Try filling with vanilla buttercream for a sweeter Swiss roll.

This Swiss roll uses a light genoise sponge with a subtle vanilla flavour. It is perfectly soft and delicate – a lovely change from traditional sponge cake!

1. Preheat the oven to 180°C (350°F) fan. Grease a 33 x 25cm (13 x 10 inch) baking tray with vegan butter and line with baking parchment.

2. Put the aquafaba and cream of tartar in the bowl of a stand mixer and mix on medium–high speed until stiff peaks are formed. This means the aquafaba doesn't move, even when tipped upside down. (If you don't have a stand mixer you can do this in a large mixing bowl with an electric hand whisk.)

3. Meanwhile, put the soya milk in a jug and heat in the microwave for 1 minute to warm through (alternatively you can do this in a pan on the hob). Once warmed, mix in the apple cider vinegar and place to the side to curdle – this will take about 5 minutes.

4. Put the flour, sugar, salt, baking powder and bicarbonate of soda in a large mixing bowl. Mix with a balloon whisk until fully combined.

5. Add the oil, vanilla and the curdled milk to the dry ingredients and mix until fully combined. The mixture will be very stiff and dry at this point, but that's normal.

6. Gently fold the aquafaba into the mixture, one spoonful at a time, trying not to knock out too much air. It will become a much looser mixture as you add more aquafaba.

7. Pour the mixture into the lined baking tray and level out the top until smooth. Bake for 15–18 minutes until a skewer comes out clean.

8. Whilst the sponge is baking, lay out a piece of baking parchment the size of the sponge and cover it with a generous sprinkle of caster sugar.

Continued overleaf...

9.   Once the sponge is baked, let it stand for a minute or so until the tin is cool enough to touch, then tip the sponge out, top-side-down, onto the sugar-covered parchment. Gently remove the baking parchment from the bottom of the sponge, then cover with a damp tea towel and leave to cool (this stops the sponge from drying out).

10. Meanwhile, whip the vegan cream and icing sugar together until the cream holds stiff peaks. I use a stand mixer but an electric whisk or balloon whisk will also work.

11. Once the sponge is cool, use a sharp knife to make an incision line widthways across the sponge, 2.5cm (1 inch) in from one of the short sides, cutting only halfway into the sponge and not all the way through (this just makes it easier to roll).

12. Spread the jam evenly across the whole of the sponge, followed by the cream on top. Use the baking parchment to help you confidently roll up the sponge from the short side where the incision was made. If there are a few cracks in the sponge, don't panic – it still tastes just as good! Cut the ends off the Swiss roll to give a professional finish, and serve with fresh raspberries, if you wish. Enjoy!

For the sponge:

vegan butter, for greasing

150g (5½oz) aquafaba (see page 149)

¼ tsp cream of tartar

90ml (3fl oz) soya milk

1 tbsp apple cider vinegar

200g (7oz) plain (all-purpose) flour

190g (6¾oz) caster (granulated) sugar, plus a sprinkle for rolling

½ tsp salt

½ tsp baking powder

¼ tsp bicarbonate of soda (baking soda)

75ml (2½fl oz) vegetable oil

1 tbsp vanilla extract

For the filling:

100ml (3½fl oz) vegan double (heavy) cream (I like Oatly Whippable)

25g (1oz) icing (confectioners') sugar

100–150g (3½–5½oz) raspberry jam (see page 169 or use shop-bought) depending on how much you prefer

fresh raspberries, to decorate (optional)

Serves 10

CHOCOLATE FUDGE CUPCAKES

Bake it Simple These cupcakes freeze very well, so you can make them in advance and ice them once defrosted.

I think fudge icing could possibly be one of the best creations to put on top of cupcakes. If you are looking for something indulgent but speedy, these cupcakes will become your go to bake.

1. Preheat the oven to 180°C (350°F) fan. Line a muffin tray with 12 cupcake cases.

2. Put the soya milk in a jug and heat in the microwave for 1 minute to warm through (alternatively you can do this in a pan on the hob). Once warmed, mix in the apple cider vinegar and place to the side to curdle – this will take about 5 minutes.

3. Meanwhile, put the flour, cocoa powder, sugar, coffee, bicarbonate of soda and salt in a large mixing bowl. Whisk together with a balloon whisk until fully combined.

4. Once the milk has curdled, add the oil and the vanilla to the same jug and mix. Pour the wet ingredients into the mixing bowl with the dry ingredients and whisk until fully combined and a glossy, lump-free mixture is formed – try not to over-mix the batter.

5. Divide the batter between the 12 cases and bake for 20–25 minutes, or until a skewer inserted into the centre of a cupcake comes out clean. Once baked, place the cupcakes on a cooling rack to cool completely.

6. Meanwhile, make the fudge icing. Put the butter, sugar, golden syrup and milk into a saucepan set over a low heat. Heat until the butter is melted and the sugar has dissolved. Take off the heat and beat in the cocoa powder and icing sugar. If there are small lumps of icing sugar, just use a balloon whisk to remove them. Leave to cool and it will thicken.

7. Once the cupcakes and the icing have cooled, place a spoonful of the icing onto each cupcake and smooth over with a flat knife or the back of a spoon. Enjoy!

For the cupcakes:

225ml (7¾fl oz) soya milk

1 tbsp apple cider vinegar

195g (7oz) plain (all-purpose) flour

40g (1½oz) cocoa powder

210g (7½oz) caster (granulated) sugar

1 tbsp instant coffee powder

1 tsp bicarbonate of soda (baking soda)

½ tsp salt

90ml (3fl oz) vegetable oil, or any neutral oil

1 tsp vanilla extract

For the fudge icing:

50g (1¾oz) vegan butter

30g (1oz) soft light brown sugar

25g (1oz) golden syrup (light corn syrup)

2 tbsp plant milk

20g (¾oz) cocoa powder

200g (7oz) icing (confectioners') sugar

Makes 12

SALTED CARAMEL CUPCAKES

This caramel sauce recipe requires minimal steps and doesn't involve a sugar thermometer. It is perfect not only for these cupcakes, but also for drizzling on top of things such as ice cream or brownies.

1. Preheat the oven to 180°C (350°F) fan. Line a muffin tray with 12 cupcake cases.

2. Put the soya milk in a jug and heat in the microwave for 1 minute to warm through (alternatively you can do this in a pan on the hob). Once warmed, mix in the apple cider vinegar and place to the side to curdle – this will take about 5 minutes.

3. Meanwhile, put the flour, sugar, bicarbonate of soda and salt in a large mixing bowl. Whisk together with a balloon whisk until fully combined.

4. Once the milk has curdled, add the oil and the vanilla to the same jug. Whisk this together so all of the wet ingredients are combined. Pour the wet ingredients into the dry ingredients and whisk until fully combined and a lump-free mixture is formed – try not to over-mix the batter.

5. Divide the batter between the 12 cases and bake for 20–25 minutes or until a skewer inserted into one of the cupcakes comes out clean. Once baked, place on a cooling rack to cool completely.

6. For the salted caramel sauce, put the sugar in a saucepan over a low–medium heat and heat, stirring regularly. The sugar will clump together, then eventually melt and become a lump-free liquid that is amber in colour. Once it reaches this point, add the butter and stir until fully combined. Leave on the heat for 1 minute without stirring, watching that it doesn't get too dark in colour, then slowly add the cream. Once the cream is fully combined, leave to boil without stirring for 1 minute, then take off the heat. Stir in the salt, then leave to cool a little before pouring into a jam jar to cool completely.

7. Add 3–4 tablespoons of the caramel sauce to the American buttercream to flavour it. Spoon the buttercream into a piping bag fitted with a star nozzle and pipe swirls of icing on top of each cooled cupcake. Drizzle extra caramel sauce on top of each cupcake. Enjoy!

For the cupcakes:
225ml (7¾fl oz) soya milk

1 tbsp apple cider vinegar

235g (8½oz) plain (all-purpose) flour

210g (7½oz) soft light brown sugar

1 tsp bicarbonate of soda (baking soda)

½ tsp salt

90ml (3fl oz) vegetable oil, or any neutral oil

1 tbsp vanilla extract

For the salted caramel sauce:
100g (3½oz) granulated sugar

45g (1½oz) vegan butter

60ml (2fl oz) vegan pouring cream, at room temperature

½ tsp salt (or to taste)

For the American buttercream:
½ recipe quantity of American buttercream (see page 171)

3–4 tbsp caramel sauce (see above)

Makes 12

Bake it Simple Keep an eye on how dark the sugar is getting when making the caramel sauce – the darker the colour the more bitter it will taste.

GLUTEN-FREE PUMPKIN SPICED CUPCAKES

Bake it Simple Use up your leftover pumpkin flesh from Halloween to make your own purée.

These cupcakes are a must throughout the autumn months. They will sit proudly as a centre piece at any Halloween celebration! The added pumpkin purée gives the cupcakes a moist texture, balanced by perfectly spiced cream cheese frosting.

1. Preheat the oven to 180°C (350°F) fan. Line a muffin tray with 12 cupcake cases.

2. Put the soya milk in a jug and heat in the microwave for 1 minute to warm through (alternatively you can do this in a pan on the hob). Once warmed, mix in the apple cider vinegar and place to the side to curdle – this will take about 5 minutes.

3. Meanwhile, put all of the dry ingredients into a bowl and whisk together until combined

4. Once the milk has curdled, add the oil to the same jug and mix. Pour the wet mixture into the dry ingredients and whisk until a smooth batter is formed – try not to over-mix the batter.

5. Finally, add the pumpkin purée to the batter and stir until fully combined.

6. Divide the batter between the 12 cupcake cases, filling them to around three-quarters full – they will rise once baked. I like to use an ice cream scoop to make it easier to fill the cases evenly.

7. Bake for 20–25 minutes until a skewer inserted into a cupcake comes out clean. Once baked, place the cupcakes on a cooling rack to cool completely.

8. Meanwhile, make the cream cheese icing. Cream the butter and icing sugar together with an electric hand whisk or in a stand mixer (a wooden spoon will work if you don't have an electric mixer) until light and fluffy. Add the cream cheese and cinnamon and whisk again until smooth and fully combined.

9. Once the cupcakes are cool, ice them. If you fancy piping the icing, spoon it into a piping bag with a round nozzle, and pipe swirls of icing onto each cupcake. Alternatively, you can just spread the icing onto each cupcake and enjoy!

For the cupcakes:
225ml (7¾fl oz) soya milk

1 tbsp apple cider vinegar

235g (8½oz) gluten-free self-raising flour (I use Doves Farm)

210g (7½oz) caster (granulated) sugar

1 tsp bicarbonate of soda (baking soda)

1 tsp ground cinnamon

¼ tsp ground nutmeg

¼ tsp ground ginger

½ tsp salt

90ml (3fl oz) vegetable oil, or any neutral oil

140g (5oz) pumpkin purée (canned works great)

For the cream cheese icing:
100g (3½oz) vegan butter block (supermarket baking block is fine)

400g (14oz) icing (confectioners') sugar

170g (6oz) vegan cream cheese

½ tsp ground cinnamon

Makes 12

GLUTEN-FREE LEMON AND ALMOND CUPCAKES

The added ground almonds give this sponge a moist texture whilst adding a subtle almond undertone. The sharp lemon curd cuts through the sweetness perfectly, marrying the two flavours together.

1. Preheat the oven to 180°C (350°F) fan. Line a muffin tray with 10 cupcake cases.

2. Put the soya milk in a jug and heat in the microwave for 1 minute to warm through (alternatively you can do this in a pan on the hob). Once warmed, mix in the apple cider vinegar and place to the side to curdle – this will take about 5 minutes.

3. Meanwhile, put the flour, ground almonds, sugar, bicarbonate of soda and lemon zest in a large bowl and whisk until combined.

4. Once the soya milk has curdled, add the oil and vanilla to the same jug and mix. Pour the wet mixture into the dry ingredients and whisk together until fully combined.

5. Divide the mixture between the 10 muffin cases and bake for 25–30 minutes, until a skewer inserted into a cupcake comes out clean. Once baked, place the cupcakes on a cooling rack to cool completely.

6. For the candied lemon slices, put 200ml (7fl oz) water and the sugar into a saucepan set over a medium heat. Cut the lemon slices in half, then add to the pan. Bring the water to a boil and simmer for 10–15 minutes until the slices look transparent. Remove from the pan and allow to dry out slightly on a piece of baking parchment before rolling in caster sugar to finish.

7. Make the buttercream using the quantities opposite and following the directions on page 171, adding in the lemon juice instead of the plant milk and vanilla. Spoon the buttercream into a piping bag fitted with a star nozzle.

8. Once the cupcakes have cooled, core out the centre of each cake using a sharp knife to make room to fill with lemon curd. Dollop 1 teaspoon of lemon curd into the centre of each cake, then pipe the top with a swirl of the buttercream. Top each cake with a candied lemon slice. Enjoy!

For the cupcakes:

225ml (7¾fl oz) soya milk

1 tbsp apple cider vinegar

135g (4¾oz) gluten-free self-raising flour (I use Doves Farm)

100g (3½oz) ground almonds

210g (7½oz) caster (granulated) sugar

¾ tsp bicarbonate of soda (baking soda)

zest of 2 large lemons

90ml (3fl oz) vegetable oil

1 tsp vanilla extract

1 tsp lemon curd per cupcake (see page 170)

For the lemon American buttercream:

125g (4½oz) vegan butter block

250g (9oz) icing (confectioners') sugar

juice of 1 lemon

For the candied lemon slices:

200g (7oz) granulated sugar

2 lemons, thinly sliced

Makes 10

BLUEBERRY MUFFINS

Bake it Simple If blueberries aren't your favourite, try using raspberries or blackberries instead.

These muffins are perfect for breakfast or as a snack with a cup of tea. They last well in a sealed container, so you can enjoy them throughout the week.

1. Preheat the oven to 220°C (425°F) fan. Line a cupcake pan with 10 large muffin cases.

2. Put the plant milk in a jug and heat in the microwave for 1 minute to warm through (alternatively you can do this in a pan on the hob). Once warmed, mix in the apple cider vinegar and place to the side to curdle – this will take about 5 minutes.

3. Meanwhile, whisk together the flour, sugar, baking powder, salt and orange zest in a large bowl.

4. Sprinkle a teaspoon of the dry ingredients over the blueberries, tossing them until they are all lightly floured to stop them from sinking to the bottom of the muffins.

5. Once the milk has curdled, add the oil, yogurt and vanilla extract to the same jug and mix. Whisk the wet ingredients into the dry until just combined, trying not to over-mix. Finally, fold in the majority of the blueberries, keeping a handful aside.

6. Divide the mixture between the 10 muffin cases; this will make large muffins so the mix will nearly fill each case. Alternatively, you can make 12 smaller muffins. Once the mixture is divided evenly, top the cases with the reserved blueberries.

7. Bake for 5 minutes at 220°C (425°F) fan, then turn the temperature down to 190°C (375°) fan and bake for a further 15–18 minutes until golden and a skewer comes out clean. Once baked, leave to cool on a cooling rack. Enjoy!

240ml (8fl oz) plant milk (preferably soya)

1 tsp apple cider vinegar

250g (9oz) plain (all-purpose) flour

150g (5½oz) caster (granulated) sugar

2 tsp baking powder

½ tsp salt

zest of 1 orange

80ml (2½fl oz) vegetable oil

70g (2½oz) vegan plain yogurt

1 tbsp vanilla extract

150g (5½oz) blueberries (fresh or frozen)

Makes 10

'NOTELLA'- FILLED MUFFINS

These muffins remind me of the ones you buy at the supermarket, with soft sponge on the bottom and a slightly crunchy top where the batter has overflowed the cases. These are made even better with a soft chocolate-hazelnut centre.

1. Preheat the oven to 180°C (350°F) fan. Line a muffin tray with 10 cupcake cases.

2. Put the soya milk in a jug and heat in the microwave for 1 minute to warm through (alternatively you can do this in a pan on the hob). Once warmed, mix in the apple cider vinegar and place to the side to curdle – this will take about 5 minutes.

3. Put the flour, cocoa powder, sugar, coffee, bicarbonate of soda and salt in a large mixing bowl and mix with a balloon whisk until fully combined.

4. Once the plant milk has curdled, add the oil and vanilla to the same jug and whisk until combined. Add the wet ingredients to the dry ingredients, along with the apple sauce. Whisk until all the ingredients are well combined, then add the chocolate chips and stir until evenly distributed.

5. Divide half of the batter between the 10 muffin cases so that they are half filled, then dollop a teaspoon of the vegan hazelnut spread into the centre of each muffin case. Use the remaining batter to cover the spread and fill the muffin cases.

6. Bake for 25 minutes, or until a skewer inserted into one of the cupcakes comes out clean. Once baked, remove from the oven and leave on a cooling rack to cool completely. Enjoy!

240ml (8fl oz) soya milk

1 tbsp apple cider vinegar

210g (7½oz) plain (all-purpose) flour

50g (1¾oz) cocoa powder

200g (7oz) soft light brown sugar

1 tbsp instant coffee powder

1 tsp bicarbonate of soda (baking soda)

½ tsp salt

80ml (2½fl oz) vegetable oil

1 tsp vanilla extract

60g (2oz) apple sauce

175g (6oz) vegan chocolate chips

1 tsp vegan chocolate-hazelnut spread for each muffin

Makes 10 large muffins

Cookies

Cookies are one of my favourite things to make as they are so easy to share with friends but don't take too much hassle. Throughout this chapter there are recipes for every type of cookie, and the majority of recipes you can change up with your favourite ingredients or things you generally have in the house. The recipes all include the yield, but it is entirely up to you how big you make the cookies. The gingerbread dough can even be used to make a gingerbread house at Christmas – all the cookie doughs are extremely versatile. You can also double up the quantities of these recipes without the fear of things not coming out the same: they will be just as perfect.

BRANDY SNAPS WITH CHANTILLY CREAM

Bake it Simple Fill the brandy snaps just before serving as the cream will make them soggy and they will lose their crunch.

The crunch of a brandy snap is unbeatable, and the warm ginger spice adds depth to the flavour. Chantilly cream is simply slightly sweetened whipped cream, which is the perfect accompaniment to this biscuit. The glacé ginger is a nice touch to tie in all the flavours.

1. Preheat the oven to 160°C (315°F) fan. Line two baking trays with baking parchment.

2. For the brandy snaps, put the butter, sugar and golden syrup in a saucepan over a low–medium heat until the butter is melted and all ingredients are fully combined.

3. Once melted, sift in the ginger and flour, then mix thoroughly until all ingredients are combined.

4. You should be able to fit four to six brandy snaps on each tray, but I would recommend you do four at a time as there is a short window between taking them out of the oven and rolling them up before they become too cool to roll. For each brandy snap, spoon 1–2 teaspoons of the mixture onto the lined tray, leaving plenty of space between them as they spread a lot in the oven.

5. Place the first tray in the oven and bake for 8–10 minutes. Once they are lacy and golden, take them out of the oven and let them stand for a minute. They don't want to be rolled straight out of the oven or they will collapse. Once set a little but whilst still warm, roll the brandy snaps, one at a time, around the handle of a wooden spoon, then place onto a cooling rack to cool. Repeat to cook the rest of the batter – you can stagger the timings if you like, putting the next tray in halfway through cooking the previous one, or just bake one tray at a time.

6. For the Chantilly cream, put the cream and icing sugar into the bowl of a stand mixer, if you have one – or into a large mixing bowl if you are using an electric hand whisk – and whisk until the cream is thick and holds stiff peaks. Fold in the glacé ginger chunks, then place the cream into a piping bag fitted with a round nozzle that is small enough to fit inside the brandy snap.

7. Once the brandy snaps are cooled, pipe the cream inside to finish. Enjoy!

For the brandy snaps:

75g (2½oz) vegan butter

75g (2½oz) soft light brown sugar

75g (2½oz) golden syrup (light corn syrup)

1 tbsp ground ginger

75g (2½oz) plain (all-purpose) flour

For the Chantilly cream:

125ml (4½fl oz) vegan double (heavy) cream (I like the Oatly Whippable as it stays very thick)

25g (1oz) icing (confectioners') sugar

50g (1¾oz) glacé ginger, chopped into fine dice

Makes 14–16

NEW YORK-STYLE COOKIES

Bake it Simple You could also fill the cookies with a small biscuit of your choice if you don't have any spread.

I had never had a thick NYC-style cookie before my friend asked me to make some for her. They are not readily available in the UK, so these are exactly how I imagine they would be if I'd had a real one. I like to fill them with a teaspoon of spread, like vegan chocolate or Biscoff spread.

1. Line two baking trays with baking parchment.

2. Scoop a teaspoon of the spread for each cookie and place it on a small plate. Pop this in the freezer whilst you make the cookie dough.

3. Put the butter and both sugars in the bowl of a stand mixer, if you have one – or into a large mixing bowl if you are using an electric hand whisk – and cream together until light in colour and fluffy. Add the vanilla and mix until fully incorporated.

4. Add all the remaining ingredients except the chocolate chunks and mix to a rough cookie dough. Add the chocolate chunks and mix until evenly distributed.

5. Divide the cookie dough into eight balls. Flatten the ball of dough, then take one of the frozen teaspoons of spread and form it into a ball. Place it into the centre of the cookie dough and enclose the dough around it so that no spread is visible. Repeat to fill the remaining seven cookies.

6. Place all the dough balls onto a lined baking tray and place in the freezer for 30 minutes. Meanwhile, preheat the oven to 180°C (350°F) fan.

7. Split the cookies between the two lined trays so there are four on each. Bake for 15–18 minutes until lightly golden on the edges. Remove from the oven and allow to cool completely on the trays. To finish you can drizzle the top with some melted spread. Enjoy!

vegan chocolate spread or Biscoff spread, plus extra to drizzle

150g (5½oz) vegan butter

100g (3½oz) soft light brown sugar

75g (2½oz) granulated sugar

1 tsp vanilla extract

250g (9oz) plain (all-purpose) flour

50g (1¾oz) cornflour (cornstarch)

1½ tsp baking powder

½ tsp bicarbonate of soda (baking soda)

2 tbsp plant milk

½ tsp salt

200g (7oz) vegan chocolate chunks

Makes 8

Bake it Simple If you don't have vegan condensed milk handy, you can use a simple American buttercream instead (see page 171).

COFFEE KISSES

I have fond memories of making coffee kisses with my gran every Sunday, especially when the weather was bad and we stayed inside to avoid the rain. They are one of the cheapest biscuits to make as they require so few ingredients. Bear in mind we didn't sandwich them with Russian buttercream, but I think the silky, slightly less sweet icing works even better than American buttercream.

1. Preheat the oven to 180°C (350°F) fan. Line two baking trays with baking parchment.

2. Put the flour, sugar and coffee powder in a large bowl and mix. Rub in the vegan butter with your fingertips until it resembles rough breadcrumbs. Add the milk and mix until it forms a smooth dough.

3. Divide the mixture into small balls around the size of a large cherry – it makes around 16 balls, depending on how large you make them. Place them onto the lined baking trays, then bake for 13–15 minutes until lightly golden on the edges. Once baked, remove from the oven and leave to cool on the trays.

4. For the Russian buttercream, put the butter in the bowl of a stand mixer, if you have one – or into a large mixing bowl if you are using an electric hand whisk – and mix on high until it is very pale in colour and fluffy. You don't want to rush this step; mix it for at least 10 minutes. Once the butter is light and fluffy, slowly add the condensed milk, 2 tablespoons at a time, allowing it to combine fully between each addition.

5. Once all of the condensed milk has been added, add the coffee powder. Finally, add the icing sugar, beating until a smooth shiny buttercream is formed. Spoon into a piping bag fitted with a star nozzle.

6. Once the biscuits have cooled, pipe rosettes of buttercream onto the flat underside of half the biscuits, then sandwich with the other half. Enjoy!

For the biscuits:

150g (5½oz) self-raising flour

75g (2½oz) caster (granulated) sugar

1 tbsp instant coffee powder

75g (2½oz) vegan butter

50ml (1¾fl oz) plant milk

For the Russian buttercream:

60g (2oz) good-quality vegan butter (Flora Plant Butter works great)

90g (3¼oz) vegan condensed milk

1–2 tsp instant coffee powder

12g (⅓oz) icing (confectioners') sugar

Makes 8–10

GINGERBREAD BISCUITS

Bake it Simple This batch of royal icing makes more than enough to decorate the biscuits, so you can play around with loads of designs.

These decorative biscuits are perfect for every season; whether you are making snowflakes at Christmas time to give as gifts to family, or making love hearts for Valentine's Day, you can't go wrong. This royal icing is the perfect consistency for piping intricate details, or get the kids involved to make their own designs!

1. Preheat the oven to 180°C (350°F) fan. Line two baking trays with baking parchment.

2. Put the butter, dark muscovado sugar and golden syrup in a saucepan over a low–medium heat until the butter is melted.

3. Sift the flour, bicarbonate of soda, ginger and cinnamon into a large bowl and mix. Pour the wet ingredients into the dry and mix until a dough is formed.

4. Split the dough in half and roll one half out on a flour-dusted surface – or between two sheets of baking parchment – until it is around 5mm (¼ inch) thick. Cut out whatever shape you'd like the biscuits to be (I used a large star cutter) and transfer them to a lined baking tray. Gather up the excess and re-roll until you have a full tray of biscuits. Repeat with the second half of the dough to fill the other baking tray.

5. Bake for 8–12 minutes until the biscuits feel firm – they will set as they cool.

6. For the royal icing, put the aquafaba and cream of tartar in the bowl of a stand mixer, if you have one – or into a large mixing bowl if you are using an electric hand whisk – and whisk on high until it reaches stiff peaks (meaning it doesn't slide about in the bowl when tipped upside down.) Once it reaches this stage, add the icing sugar, a tablespoon at a time, until you have a stiff glossy icing. Divide the icing into bowls and colour as desired or leave it white.

7. Place the icing into piping bags and decorate the cooled gingerbread biscuits however you like! Enjoy!

For the biscuits:
125g (4½oz) vegan butter

100g (3½oz) dark muscovado sugar

50g (1¾oz) golden syrup (light corn syrup)

300g (10½oz) plain (all-purpose) flour

1 tsp bicarbonate of soda (baking soda)

1 heaped tbsp ground ginger

½ tsp ground cinnamon

For the royal icing:
6 tbsp aquafaba (see page 149)

¼ tsp cream of tartar

250g (9oz) icing (confectioners') sugar

food colouring (optional)

Makes 8–12 depending on the size of your cutter

LEMON
VIENNESE
WHIRLS

Bake it Simple If you don't want to make lemon curd, use vanilla buttercream and cover half of the Viennese whirl in dark chocolate.

These biscuits are so soft and buttery, they literally melt in your mouth. They look like they require lots of effort but take little to no time to make.

1. Line two baking trays with baking parchment.

2. Put the butter and icing sugar into the bowl of a stand mixer, if you have one – or into a large mixing bowl if you are using an electric hand whisk – and beat together until light in colour and fluffy. Add the vanilla and salt and mix until fully incorporated.

3. Add the flour, cornflour, baking powder and lemon zest, and mix until just combined and a smooth dough is formed – try not to over-mix.

4. Transfer the dough to a piping bag fitted with a star nozzle and pipe swirls of the dough onto the lined baking trays. You should be able to pipe between 12–16 biscuits from the batter. Place the trays into the freezer for 30 minutes before baking – this will ensure they hold their shape when baked. Meanwhile, preheat the oven to 160°C (315°F) fan.

5. Once the biscuits have had their time in the freezer, bake them for 12 minutes, or until they are lightly golden on the edges – they don't want to be dark in colour. Once baked, remove from the oven and leave to cool fully on the trays.

6. Meanwhile, make the American buttercream using the quantity opposite and following the directions on page 171, adding the lemon juice. Spoon it into a piping bag fitted with a star nozzle.

7. Once the biscuits are cool, pipe a swirl of buttercream onto half of the biscuits, then spread a teaspoon of lemon curd onto the other half. Sandwich the biscuits together so they are filled with both lemon curd and buttercream. Enjoy!

For the biscuits:
200g (7oz) vegan butter, at room temperature

50g (1¾oz) icing (confectioners') sugar

1 tsp vanilla extract

a pinch of salt

200g (7oz) plain (all-purpose) flour

15g (½oz) cornflour (cornstarch)

½ tsp baking powder

zest of 2 lemons

For the filling:
½ recipe quantity of American buttercream (see page 171)

juice of 1 lemon

6–8 tsp vegan lemon curd (see page 170, or use shop-bought)

Makes 6–8

Bake it Simple You
can roll the biscuits
in desiccated
coconut instead of
oats, if you prefer.

MELTING MOMENTS

These are another of my gran's favourites. I was slightly sceptical about the vegan version tasting the same, but I can reassure you it does. The soft buttery biscuits literally melt in your mouth – it makes it impossible to just eat one!

1. Preheat the oven to 160°C (315°F) fan. Line a large baking tray or two smaller ones with baking parchment.

2. Put the butter and sugar into the bowl of a stand mixer, if you have one – or into a large mixing bowl if you are using an electric hand whisk – and cream together until light and fluffy. Add the milk and vanilla and mix until fully incorporated. Sift in the flour and mix until just combined and a smooth dough is formed – try not to overmix.

3. Take spoonfuls of the mixture and roll into balls – they should be slightly smaller than a golf ball to make 12 biscuits.

4. Put the oats in a shallow bowl, then roll each ball of dough in the oats until covered. Place the oaty balls on the lined baking tray and flatten slightly. Place a glacé cherry half on top of each biscuit.

5. Bake for 10–15 minutes until lightly golden on the edges. Leave to cool on the tray, then enjoy!

120g (4¼oz) vegan butter

80g (2¾oz) caster (granulated) sugar

50ml (1¾fl oz) plant milk

2 tsp vanilla extract

180g (6¼oz) self-raising flour

a large handful of oats

6 glacé cherries, halved

Makes 12

RAISIN OATMEAL COOKIES

Bake it Simple **Add your favourite chopped nuts for an extra crunch.**

These are the type of cookies that feel somewhat healthy to eat even though they probably aren't at all. They are packed with chewy raisins and have crispy golden edges along with a dash of cinnamon... who cares if they are healthy anyway!

1. Preheat the oven to 180°C (350°F) fan. Line two baking trays with baking parchment.

2. Put the butter and both sugars in the bowl of a stand mixer, if you have one – or into a large mixing bowl if you are using an electric hand whisk – and cream together until light in colour and fluffy. Once fully combined, mix in the vanilla, salt and plant milk.

3. In a bowl, combine the flour, oats and cinnamon, then add this to the butter and sugar mixture. Mix well until the ingredients are fully combined, then finally mix in the raisins until they are evenly distributed.

4. Divide the mixture into balls, around the size of golf balls, and place onto the lined baking trays, leaving a small gap between each. Gently press each cookie down to flatten slightly, then bake for 12–15 minutes until lightly golden on the edges. Leave to cool on the tray. Enjoy!

115g (4oz) vegan butter

100g (3½oz) soft light brown sugar

50g (1¾oz) granulated sugar

1 tsp vanilla extract

a pinch of salt

50ml (1¾fl oz) plant milk

125g (4½oz) self-raising flour

150g (5½oz) porridge oats

1 tsp ground cinnamon

150g (5½oz) raisins

Makes 14–16

YORKSHIRE RASCALS

Bake it Simple You can serve these simply with vegan butter, or as you would a traditional scone with jam and vegan cream!

Depending on where you are from, you may have never heard of a 'fat rascal' before. They are inspired by the ones at Bettys, the famous tea room in Yorkshire, and have been a true family favourite since before I can remember – I see them as an upgraded version of a traditional scone. They are packed full of fruit and have a subtle cinnamon flavour. You really need to give them a try.

1. Preheat the oven to 200°C (400°F) fan. Line a large baking tray with baking parchment.

2. Pour the soya milk into a jug, add the lemon juice, stir, then set aside to curdle.

3. Put the plain flour, self-raising flour and baking powder in a large bowl and mix together. Rub in the cubed butter with your fingertips until it resembles rough breadcrumbs. Add the sugar, cinnamon, mixed fruit and zests, then mix until fully combined and the fruit is evenly distributed.

4. Once the soya milk has curdled, add the crème fraîche or yogurt to the same jug and whisk together. Add this to the dry ingredients and mix together until it forms a dough. Start with a wooden spoon, but you will probably need to use your hands at the end to bring it together.

5. Tip the dough out onto a floured work surface and roll out until it is around 2cm (¾ inch) thick. Cut out rounds using an 8cm (3¼ inch) cutter, gather up the excess and repeat until you have eight fat rascals. Place onto the lined baking tray and brush the tops with soya milk. Press two glacé cherry halves and two blanched almonds onto each rascal.

6. Bake for 15–20 minutes until golden brown on top. Leave to cool on a cooling rack. Enjoy!

180ml (6fl oz) soya milk, plus extra for glazing

1 tbsp lemon juice

200g (7oz) plain (all-purpose) flour, plus extra for dusting

200g (7oz) self-raising flour

1 tsp baking powder

100g (3½oz) cold vegan butter, diced

125g (4½oz) soft light brown sugar

2 tsp ground cinnamon

150g (5½oz) mixed fruit

zest of 1 lemon

zest of 1 orange

50g (1¾oz) vegan crème fraîche or plain vegan yogurt

8 glacé cherries, halved

16 blanched almonds

Makes 8

JAMMY HEARTS

Bake it Simple
I sometimes like to fill these with a little vanilla buttercream around the edge of the jam, too. See page 171 for the buttercream recipe.

I love to make these around Valentine's Day to feel festive, even if I just eat them all myself! They do look even more special if you put them in a little cardboard box and tie with a ribbon: the perfect present!

1. Preheat the oven to 160°C (315°F) fan. Line two baking trays with baking parchment.

2. Put the butter and icing sugar into the bowl of a stand mixer, if you have one – or into a large mixing bowl if you are using an electric hand whisk – and beat together until light in colour and fluffy. Add the vanilla and salt and mix until fully incorporated.

3. Sift in the flour and cornflour, then mix until a smooth dough is formed.

4. Roll out the dough, either on a floured work surface or between two sheets of parchment, until it is around 5mm (¼ inch) thick. It doesn't want to be too thick as the biscuits will be sandwiched together. Cut out around 24 biscuits using a heart-shaped cutter, or a round one if that's all you have. The size of your cutter will determine the number of biscuits you make.

5. Place the biscuits onto the lined baking trays, then use a smaller heart-shaped cutter to cut out the centre of half of the biscuits. Bake for 15–18 minutes until very slightly golden around the edges – they should still be light in colour and they will firm up as they cool. Once baked, leave to cool fully on the tray.

6. Once the biscuits are cool, spread a dollop of jam onto the biscuits without the heart cut out of the middle. Sandwich the second biscuit (the one with the heart cut out) on top so the jam is peeking through. Enjoy!

For the shortbread:
250g (9oz) vegan butter

140g (5oz) icing (confectioners') sugar

1 tbsp vanilla extract

a pinch of salt

250g (9oz) plain (all-purpose) flour

140g (5oz) cornflour (cornstarch)

For the filling:
150g (5½oz) smooth raspberry jam (see page 169, or use shop-bought)

Makes 12–14

TRIPLE CHOCOLATE COOKIES

Bake it Simple Replace the cocoa powder with more self-raising flour for a simple chocolate chip cookie.

These have to be the most versatile cookies you could make – pop them in the microwave for 30 seconds and serve with a scoop of ice cream for the perfect dessert, or fill with a swirl of buttercream for a cookie sandwich.

1. Preheat oven 180°C (350°F) fan. Line two baking trays with baking parchment.

2. Put the butter and sugar in the bowl of a stand mixer, if you have one – or into a large mixing bowl if you are using an electric hand whisk – and cream together until light in colour and fluffy. Once fully combined, mix in the vanilla, salt and plant milk.

3. Add the flour and cocoa powder and mix to a rough cookie dough. Finally, add the two types of chocolate chunks and mix until evenly distributed.

4. Divide the dough into equal 10 portions – you can make more or less depending on how large you'd like the cookies to be – and roll each into a ball.

5. Place five balls of dough onto each baking tray and bake for 15–20 minutes until lightly golden on the edges. Leave to cool on the tray, then enjoy!

120g (4¼oz) vegan butter

220g (7¾oz) caster (granulated) sugar

1 tsp vanilla extract

½ tsp salt

50ml (1¾fl oz) plant milk

200g (7oz) self-raising flour

25g (1oz) cocoa powder

75g (2½oz) vegan dark chocolate chunks

75g (2½oz) vegan white chocolate chunks

Makes 10

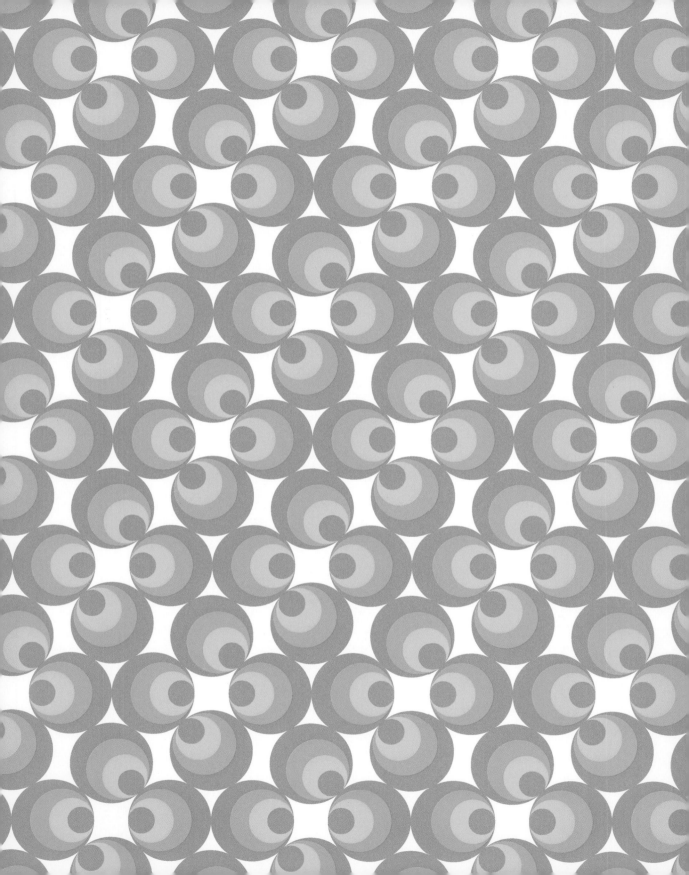

Bread

I have included instructions for making these bread recipes with and without a stand mixer fitted with a dough hook. The bread will still come out just as delicious without a mixer, but it takes a little more effort to knead things by hand. If you aren't using a mixer, be patient and keep kneading the bread until it feels smooth and elastic, generally at least 10 minutes. A good test to know if the bread has been kneaded enough and the gluten has relaxed is the windowpane test: if you hold up a piece of the dough near a window and stretch it gently, you want to be able to see the light coming through without the dough tearing. The recipes call for leaving the dough in a warm place to prove (I use my airing cupboard at home), preferably somewhere that doesn't have a draught. Finally, instead of using plastic wrap to cover my dough, to reduce waste I use a clean, clear shower cap... it works great!

CINNAMON ROLLS

Cinnamon rolls have a special place in my heart as they were the first thing Lizzie and I baked together after Bake Off and are still, to this day, our favourite thing to bake together. These are so good enjoyed freshly baked, or if they are a day old, they taste even better warmed up in the microwave.

1. Grease a 36 x 26cm (14 x 10½ inch) traybake tin with butter and line with a piece of baking parchment.

2. Put the milk and butter into a pan over a low heat until the butter is just melted. Pour into a bowl and let cool to lukewarm – it doesn't want to be cold, but if it's too hot it will kill the yeast. Add the yeast to the milk, stir, then leave to the side for 10 minutes to get foamy.

3. In the bowl of a stand mixer fitted with a dough hook, mix together the flour, sugar and salt. If you don't have a mixer, use a large mixing bowl and wooden spoon. Add the milk and yeast mixture to the dry ingredients and mix on low speed, or by hand, for 5 minutes until fully incorporated. Turn the speed up to medium and mix for another 5 minutes until the dough is smooth and elastic. This will take around 10 minutes to knead by hand. If you hold a piece of the dough up to the light, you should see the light through when you stretch it without it tearing. Knead until you reach this stage.

4. Place the dough in an oiled bowl, cover with a reusable cover, shower cap or plastic wrap and leave to prove in a warm place for 1 hour, or until doubled in size.

5. Meanwhile, for the filling, beat together the butter and sugar until fully combined, then mix in the cinnamon.

6. Once the dough has proved, tip it out onto a lightly floured work surface, or a non-stick mat if you have one. Roll it out to a rectangle measuring roughly 45 x 35cm (18 x 14 inches). Spread the filling evenly across the dough, spreading right to the edges. Roll up from the long side, positioning the seam underneath the log. Trim off the two ends, then cut into 12 equal pieces.

7. Arrange the cinnamon rolls, cut sides up, into the traybake tin. Cover and leave to prove for another hour. Meanwhile, preheat the oven to 180°C (350°F) fan.

8. Once proved, bake the rolls for 20–25 minutes, until lightly golden on the edges.

9. For the icing, mix the icing sugar with 2–3 tablespoons water until smooth, then transfer to a piping bag. Once the cinnamon rolls are cool, pipe over the icing to finish. Enjoy!

For the dough:
275ml (9½fl oz) soya milk

100g (3½oz) vegan butter, plus extra for greasing

7g (¼oz) fast action dried yeast

550g (1lb 4oz) strong white bread flour

60g (2oz) caster (granulated) sugar

½ tsp salt

oil, for greasing

For the filling:
80g (2¾oz) vegan butter, softened

160g (5¾oz) soft light brown sugar

3 tbsp ground cinnamon

For the icing:
200g (7oz) icing (confectioners') sugar

Makes 12

Bake it Simple You can use the cream cheese frosting from the Carrot Cake (see page 16) if you like your cinnamon rolls with cream cheese.

CHOCOLATE HAZELNUT BABKA

Bake it Simple If you want to make this even easier, use shop-bought vegan chocolate spread for the filling and just add some chopped roasted hazelnuts.

Babka was one of my discoveries after watching *The Great British Bake Off*. When I saw it being made on the show, I was desperate to try a vegan version. This soft bread is filled to the brim with chocolate hazelnut filling and has a sticky agave glaze.

1. Grease a 450g (1lb) loaf tin with butter and line with a piece of baking parchment that hangs over the sides of the tin, or use a loaf tin liner if you have one.

2. Put the soya milk into a jug and heat in the microwave for about 30 seconds until lukewarm – it doesn't want to be cold, but if it's too hot it will kill the yeast. Alternatively, you can do this in a pan on the hob. Add the yeast to the milk, stir, then leave to the side for 10 minutes to get foamy.

3. In the bowl of a stand mixer fitted with a dough hook, mix together the flour, sugar and salt. If you don't have a mixer, use a large mixing bowl and wooden spoon. Add the milk and yeast mixture to the dry ingredients and mix on low speed, or by hand, for around 3 minutes until combined. Turn the speed up to medium and slowly add the softened butter, one cube at a time, until fully incorporated – this will take around 5 minutes; be patient as it will eventually come together. Mix for a further 5 minutes until the dough is smooth and elastic, or knead by hand for 10 minutes if you don't have a mixer.

4. Place the dough in an oiled bowl, cover with a reusable cover, shower cap or plastic wrap and leave to prove in a warm place for 1 hour, or until doubled in size.

5. Meanwhile, for the filling, add the hazelnuts to a food processor and blend until it forms a nut butter. Add the melted chocolate, syrup, vanilla and salt and mix until combined and a smooth spread forms.

6. Once the dough has proved, tip it out onto a lightly floured work surface, or a non-stick mat if you have one. Roll it out to a rectangle measuring roughly 40 x 30cm (16 x 12 inches). Spread the filling out across the dough, then sprinkle over the chopped toasted hazelnuts. Roll up the dough from the longest side into a tight Swiss roll, positioning the seam underneath the log.

7. Trim off the two ends to make it neater, then use a sharp knife to cut through the middle of the log lengthways so that you get two long pieces of dough. Lay them next to each other, cut sides up, and pinch the top of the two pieces together. Twist the two lengths together to create a two stranded plait, then pinch to seal the two pieces together at the bottom too. Place the bread into the lined loaf tin, cover and leave to prove for another 30–45 minutes, or until puffy. Meanwhile, preheat the oven to 180°C (350°F) fan.

8. Bake for 30–35 minutes until golden brown. Cover the babka with a sheet of foil after 15 minutes to stop the top getting too brown. Once baked, remove from the oven and brush the loaf with the agave syrup to glaze. Leave to cool completely. Enjoy!

For the dough:

150ml (5fl oz) soya milk

5g (⅛oz) fast action dried yeast

275g (9¾oz) strong white bread flour, plus extra for dusting

25g (1oz) caster (granulated) sugar

½ tsp salt

80g (2¾oz) vegan butter, softened, plus extra for greasing

oil, for greasing

1 tbsp agave syrup, to glaze

For the filling:

100g (3½oz) blanched hazelnuts

50g (1¾oz) vegan dark chocolate, melted

2–4 tbsp golden syrup (light corn syrup)

½ tsp vanilla extract

a pinch of salt

1 x 100g (3½oz) bag chopped toasted hazelnuts

Serves 10–12

FRUIT LOAF

Bake it Simple I am very Yorkshire, so I like to use Yorkshire Tea, but Earl Grey also works well.

This light, slightly sweet loaf is jam-packed with fruit. It is perfect served freshly baked or toasted with lashings of vegan butter at breakfast time. Add in whatever dried fruit you have around the house.

1. Put the milk and butter into a pan over a low heat until the butter is just melted. Pour into a bowl and allow to cool to lukewarm – it doesn't want to be cold, but if it's too hot it will kill the yeast. Add the yeast to the milk, stir, then leave to the side for 10 minutes to get foamy.

2. Pour the freshly boiled water into a jug, then add the tea bag, the mixed fruit and dried apricots, stir and leave to brew for 10 minutes.

3. Meanwhile, put the flour, spices, sugar, salt and orange zest in a large bowl and mix.

4. Drain the water from the fruit (I generally just use a sieve) and discard the tea bag, then add the fruit to the dry ingredients, along with the yeast and milk mixture, and mix until fully incorporated and a dough forms. Tip the dough out onto a floured work surface and knead for 5–10 minutes until it is smooth and elastic.

5. Place the dough in an oiled bowl, cover with a reusable cover, shower cap or plastic wrap and leave to prove in a warm place for 45 minutes or until doubled in size. Meanwhile, grease a 450g (1lb) loaf tin with butter.

6. Place the proved dough into the tin, pressing it into the corners. Cover and leave to prove for a further 30 minutes. Preheat the oven to 180°C (350°F) fan.

7. Once risen again, brush the top of the loaf with milk, then bake for 25–30 minutes until golden brown and the loaf sounds hollow when tapped on the base. Once the tin is cool enough to touch, remove the loaf and leave to cool fully on a cooling rack. Enjoy!

200ml (7fl oz) plant milk (I use soya), plus extra for glazing

50g (1¾oz) vegan butter

7g (¼oz) fast action dried yeast

250ml (9fl oz) freshly boiled water

1 tea bag of your choice

150g (5½oz) dried mixed fruit

50g (1¾oz) chopped dried apricots

400g (14oz) strong white bread flour, plus extra for dusting

1 tsp ground cinnamon

½ tsp ground ginger

50g (1¾oz) caster (granulated) sugar

½ tsp salt

zest of 1 orange

oil, for greasing

Serves 10–12

MILK BREAD TEAR AND SHARE

Japanese milk bread is the softest, pillowy bread that you can imagine. It is perfectly sweet in flavour and I have kept it simple with a little dark chocolate as the filling. This bread is so much better than anything you can buy in the shops; it's so worth the little extra effort.

1. For the tangzhong, place the 40g (1½oz) flour and 200ml (7fl oz) water in a pan over a medium heat and whisk together so there are no lumps. Whisk until the mixture is a thick curd-like consistency, then tip it into a bowl and place in the fridge to cool. This is the bread starter.

2. Put the flour, coconut milk powder, yeast, sugar and salt into the bowl of a stand mixer fitted with a dough hook if you have one, or into a large mixing bowl if not, making sure the salt and yeast are not touching. Mix together until all of the ingredients are combined.

3. Once the tangzhong has cooled, add it to the bowl of dry ingredients, along with the milk. Mix on low until all of the ingredients are combined, then add the softened butter and mix for 5 minutes until all of the butter is fully incorporated. If you don't have a mixer, put everything in a mixing bowl and start mixing with a wooden spoon, but you might need to use your hands to make sure all of the ingredients are fully incorporated. Turn up the mixer to medium speed and mix for another 5 minutes until the dough no longer sticks to the side and feels tacky not sticky, or knead by hand for 10 minutes.

4. Place the dough in an oiled bowl, cover with a reusable cover, shower cap or plastic wrap and leave to prove in a warm place for 1 hour or until doubled in size. Line a large baking tray with baking parchment.

For the tangzhong (bread starter):
40g (1½oz) strong white bread flour

For the dough:
500g (1lb 2oz) strong white bread flour

25g (1oz) dried coconut milk powder

7g (¼oz) fast action dried yeast

45g (1½oz) caster (granulated) sugar

7g (¼oz) salt

260ml (9fl oz) soya milk, room temperature, plus extra for glazing

60g (2oz) vegan butter, cubed and softened

oil, for greasing

100g (3½oz) vegan chocolate chips

For the icing:
200g (7oz) icing (confectioners') sugar

food colouring (optional)

Serves 10

Continued overleaf...

5. Once proved, divide the dough into 10 equal pieces. On a lightly floured surface, roll each piece out into a rectangle with a rolling pin. Place some of the chocolate chips (roughly 10g [$\frac{1}{3}$oz]) on a short end and roll up like a Swiss roll, sealing the edges to make sure the chocolate is fully enclosed and using the palms of your hands to shape into a ball. Repeat to fill and shape the remaining nine pieces of dough.

6. Arrange five balls of dough in a circle on the lined baking tray, leaving around 2.5cm (1 inch) between each ball of dough so they have space to expand, and leaving a large hole in the middle so it looks like a Christmas wreath, star, or whatever shape you like. Arrange the other five balls on the outside of the circle, where each bun joins, to create a second layer of the wreath, again leaving room for them to expand, but close enough together that they will touch when baked.

7. Cover again and leave to prove for a further 30 minutes. Meanwhile, preheat the oven to 180°C (350°F) fan.

8. Once proved, brush the top of each bun with soya milk, then bake for 20–25 minutes until golden brown. Once baked, place on a cooling rack to cool completely.

9. For the icing, mix the icing sugar with 2–3 tablespoons water until smooth. Add food colouring of your choice, if wished, then drizzle over the wreath to finish. Enjoy!

CRANBERRY, PISTACHIO AND CHOCOLATE WREATH

This is a show-stopping enriched bread, perfect for sharing. Cranberries, pistachios and dark chocolate are a match made in heaven, but you can use your favourite flavours, if you'd prefer.

1. Line a large baking tray with a baking parchment. Put the milk and butter into a pan over a low heat until the butter is just melted. Pour into a bowl and allow to cool to lukewarm – it doesn't want to be cold, but if it's too hot it will kill the yeast. Add the yeast to the milk, stir, then leave to the side for 10 minutes to get foamy.

2. In a stand mixer fitted with a dough hook, combine the flour, lemon zest, salt and sugar. If you don't have a mixer, use a mixing bowl and wooden spoon. Add the yeast mixture and mix on low speed, or by hand, until incorporated. Increase the speed to medium and mix for another 5 minutes until the dough is smooth and elastic. This will take around 10 minutes to knead by hand. If you hold a piece of the dough up to the light, you should see the light through when you stretch it without it tearing. Place the dough in an oiled bowl, cover and leave to prove in a warm place for 1 hour, or until doubled in size.

3. Meanwhile, make the filling. Cream the butter and sugar together until smooth, then mix in the vanilla extract.

4. Once the dough has doubled in size, tip it out onto a lightly floured work surface. Roll it out to a rectangle measuring roughly 45 x 35cm (18 x 14 inches). Spread the filling evenly across the dough, going right to the edges, then sprinkle over the cranberries, pistachios and chocolate, reserving a little of each to sprinkle on the top later.

5. Roll up the dough from the long side into a log. Use a sharp knife to cut the log almost in half lengthways, stopping about 2.5cm (1 inch) from one end so the pieces are still connected at the top. Twist the two lengths together, so you have a two-stranded plait, then bring the ends together and seal them to create a round wreath shape. Gently place this onto the lined baking tray, cover and leave to prove for a further 45 minutes. Preheat the oven to 180°C (350°F) fan.

6. Bake the bread for 20–25 minutes until golden in colour. Once baked, remove from the oven and leave to cool.

7. For the icing, mix the icing sugar with 2–3 tablespoons water until it is thick but still pourable. Once the bread is cool, move it to a serving board, drizzle over the icing, then sprinkle over the remaining cranberries, pistachios and dark chocolate. Enjoy!

For the dough:
250ml (9fl oz) plant milk (I use soya)

50g (1¾oz) vegan butter

7g (¼oz) fast action dried yeast

500g (1lb 2oz) strong white bread flour

zest of 1 lemon

1 tsp salt

50g (1¾oz) caster (granulated) sugar

oil, for greasing

For the filling:
80g (2¾oz) vegan butter, softened

160g (5¾oz) soft light brown sugar

1 tsp vanilla extract

75g (2½oz) dried cranberries roughly chopped

75g (2½oz) pistachios, roughly chopped

100g (3½oz) vegan dark chocolate, roughly chopped

For the icing:
100g (3½oz) icing (confectioners') sugar

Serves 16

Bake it Simple **Don't worry if some of the filling seeps out of the bread when it is in the oven – once you move it onto a serving platter, you'll never know!**

ICED FINGERS

My mum and I love to get iced fingers from our local bakery and eat them whilst we walk the dogs along the beach. They are such a simple thing, a bread roll covered in water icing, yet they bring us so much joy – they are one of my favourite bakes for sure.

1. For the tangzhong, place the 30g (1oz) flour and 150ml (5fl oz) water in a pan over a medium heat and whisk together so there are no lumps. Whisk until the mixture is a thick curd-like consistency, then tip it into a bowl and place in the fridge to cool.

2. Put the flour, coconut milk powder, yeast, sugar and salt into the bowl of a stand mixer fitted with a dough hook if you have one, or into a large mixing bowl if not, making sure the salt and yeast are not touching. Mix together until all of the ingredients are combined.

3. Once the tangzhong has cooled, add it to the dry ingredients, along with the milk. Mix on low until all of the ingredients are combined, then add the softened butter and mix for 5 minutes until all of the butter is fully incorporated. If you don't have a mixer, put everything in a mixing bowl and start mixing with a wooden spoon, but you might need to use your hands to make sure all of the ingredients are fully incorporated. Turn up the mixer to medium speed and mix for another 5 minutes until the dough no longer sticks to the side and feels tacky not sticky, or knead by hand for 10 minutes.

4. Place the dough in an oiled bowl, cover with a reusable cover, shower cap or plastic wrap and leave to prove in a warm place for 1 hour or until doubled in size. Meanwhile, line two baking trays with baking parchment.

5. Once risen, split the dough into eight equal pieces. On a lightly floured surface, roll each piece out into a rectangle with a rolling pin, then roll up like a Swiss roll, starting from a short end to make a sausage shape. Now roll into a finger around 15cm (6 inches) long. Repeat to roll the remaining pieces of dough, then transfer them to the baking trays, placing four rolls on each with about a 2.5cm (1 inch) gap between them. Cover and leave to prove for a further 45 minutes. Meanwhile, preheat the oven to 175°C (350°F) fan.

6. Once proved, bake the rolls for 12–15 minutes until lightly golden brown on the top. Once baked, leave to cool on a cooling rack.

7. For the icing, mix the icing sugar with 1–2 tablespoons water until smooth, then mix in a little food colouring, if using. Once the buns are cool, either spoon over the icing and spread across the top, or dip the top of the buns straight into the icing. Leave the icing to set. Enjoy!

For the tangzhong (bread starter):
30g (1oz) strong white bread flour

For the dough:
430g (15¼oz) strong white bread flour

10g (⅓oz) dried coconut milk powder

7g (¼oz) fast action dried yeast

45g (1½oz) caster (granulated) sugar

9g (⅓oz) salt

190ml (6¾fl oz) soya milk, at room temperature

35g (1¼oz) vegan butter, softened

oil, for greasing

For the icing:
200g (7oz) icing (confectioners') sugar

food colouring (optional)

Makes 8

JAM DOUGHNUTS

I grew up by the seaside, so freshly made doughnuts have been something I've always enjoyed. Not everyone had that luxury, so I've made a recipe that reminds me of doughnuts from the beach but can be enjoyed wherever you live. They are filled to the brim with jam because that's exactly how I like them.

1. Put the soya milk in a jug and heat in the microwave for 30 seconds to warm through (alternatively you can do this in a pan on the hob). It wants to be lukewarm, but if it's too hot it will kill the yeast. Add the sugar and yeast to the milk, stir, then leave to the side for 10 minutes to get foamy.

2. In the bowl of a stand mixer fitted with a dough hook, mix together the flour and salt. If you don't have a mixer, use a large mixing bowl and wooden spoon. Add the milk and yeast mixture to the dry ingredients, along with the oil, and mix on low speed, or by hand, for 5 minutes until fully incorporated. Leave to rest for 1 minute, then mix on medium speed for another 5 minutes until the dough is smooth and elastic. This will take around 10 minutes to knead by hand.

3. Place the dough in an oiled bowl, cover with a reusable cover, shower cap or plastic wrap and leave to prove in a warm place for 1 hour. Once doubled in size, knock the dough back, re-roll it into a ball and leave to prove for another hour. Meanwhile, line a large baking tray with baking parchment.

4. Once proved, divide the dough into eight equal pieces, each weighing roughly 60g (2oz). Roll each piece into a ball, using the palm of your hands to tuck the edges underneath. Place the balls onto the lined tray, then flatten them slightly. Cover with a tea towel and leave to prove for an hour until puffy.

5. Heat the oil to between 160–170°C (315–325°F) in a deep fryer or a deep saucepan. If using a saucepan, you will need to use a jam thermometer, or similar, to test the temperature, and keep checking the temperature throughout the frying process. Fry the doughnuts, two at a time, for around 4 minutes, or until golden brown, then flip over and fry for the same amount of time on the other side. Lift the doughnuts out of the oil with a slotted spoon and place onto a piece of kitchen paper to absorb any excess oil. Leave to cool.

6. Put the sugar into a bowl, then roll the doughnuts in it until they are fully covered in sugar. Spoon the jam into a piping bag fitted with a funnel nozzle or a long round nozzle. Poke a hole in the side of the doughnut big enough for the funnel nozzle to fit inside, then fill with jam until it starts to seep out of the hole, meaning it is as full as possible. Repeat with the rest of the doughnuts. Enjoy!

For the dough:

165ml (5½fl oz) soya milk

40g (1½oz) caster (granulated) sugar

7g (¼oz) fast action dried yeast

250g (9oz) strong white bread flour

½ tsp salt

30ml (1fl oz) vegetable oil, plus extra for greasing

To fry and fill:

1L (35fl oz) vegetable oil, for frying

100g (3½oz) caster (superfine) sugar, for rolling the doughnuts in

150g (5½oz) raspberry jam (see page 169 or use shop-bought if preferred)

Makes 8

STOLLEN

This traditional German bake is generally enjoyed around Christmas time, but to be honest I sometimes make it in the summer as I enjoy it so much. The bread is crammed with fruit and a thick log of marzipan.

1. Combine the mixed fruit, apricots, glacé cherries and mixed peel in a bowl. Squeeze over the juice of the orange, add the zest and mix, then allow the fruit to sit in the juice for 10 minutes.

2. Put the milk in a jug and heat in the microwave for 30 seconds to warm through (alternatively you can do this in a pan on the hob). It wants to be lukewarm, but if it's too hot it will kill the yeast. Add the yeast to the milk, stir, then leave to the side for 10 minutes to get foamy.

3. In the bowl of a stand mixer fitted with a dough hook, mix together the flour, sugar, salt, mixed spice and chopped almonds. If you don't have a mixer, use a large mixing bowl and wooden spoon. Drain the juice from the fruit, then add this to the dry ingredients along with the yeast and milk mixture and mix on low speed, or by hand, for around 3 minutes until combined. Turn the speed up to medium and slowly add the softened butter, one cube at a time, until fully incorporated – this will take around 5 minutes; be patient as it will eventually come together. Mix for a further 5 minutes on medium–high speed until the dough comes together, or knead by hand for 10 minutes if you don't have a mixer. It will be a very wet dough, but don't worry, that's normal.

4. Place the dough into an oiled bowl, cover with a reusable cover, shower cap or plastic wrap and leave to prove in a warm place for 1 hour or until doubled in size. Meanwhile, line a large baking tray with baking parchment.

5. Once proved, tip the dough out onto a floured work surface – the dough is quite wet so you will need a little flour to stop it sticking. With a rolling pin, roll it out into a rough rectangle measuring about 20 x 30cm (8 x 12 inches), then roll the marzipan into a log shape slightly shorter than the longest side of the rectangle. Place the marzipan at the bottom of the long side of the rectangle, then roll the dough up to encase the marzipan. Seal both ends and place the loaf, seam side down, onto the baking tray. Cover and leave to prove for a further 1 hour. Preheat the oven to 180°C (350°F) fan.

6. Once proved, bake for 30 minutes or until golden on top and sounds hollow when tapped underneath. Leave to cool fully before dusting generously with icing sugar. Enjoy!

100g (3½oz) dried mixed fruit

50g (1¾oz) dried apricots, chopped

25g (1oz) glacé cherries, chopped

25g (1oz) mixed peel

juice and zest of 1 orange

175ml (5½fl oz) soya milk

7g (¼oz) fast action dried yeast

275g (9¾oz) strong white bread flour, plus extra for dusting

30g (1oz) granulated sugar

½ tsp salt

1 tsp mixed spice (apple pie spice)

50g (1¾oz) blanched almonds, chopped

50g (1¾oz) vegan butter, softened

oil, for greasing

225g (8oz) marzipan

icing (confectioners') sugar, for dusting

Serves 12

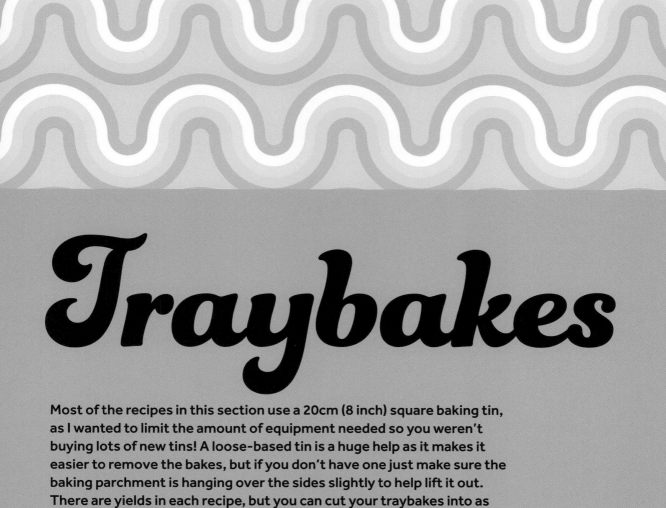

Traybakes

Most of the recipes in this section use a 20cm (8 inch) square baking tin, as I wanted to limit the amount of equipment needed so you weren't buying lots of new tins! A loose-based tin is a huge help as it makes it easier to remove the bakes, but if you don't have one just make sure the baking parchment is hanging over the sides slightly to help lift it out. There are yields in each recipe, but you can cut your traybakes into as many slices as you like. I am from Yorkshire, so I never do small portions...

THE BEST CHOCOLATE BROWNIES

Bake it Simple For a different flavoured brownie, try swirling in teaspoons of peanut butter and jam before baking.

It's fair to say I've eaten my fair share of chocolate brownies. These are the perfect balance of chewy edge, soft fudgy centre and crinkly, shiny topping. In my eyes they really are the only brownies you'll ever need to make.

1. Preheat the oven to 160°C (315°F) fan. Grease a 20cm (8 inch) square baking tin with butter and line with baking parchment.

2. Place the dark chocolate in a heatproof bowl and melt, either in the microwave for 30 second increments or over a saucepan of gently simmering water.

3. Put the aquafaba and cream of tartar in the bowl of a stand mixer, if you have one – or into a large mixing bowl if you are using an electric hand whisk – and whisk on medium–high speed until it reaches stiff peaks. Add the caster sugar a tablespoon at a time and mix until fully incorporated and you have a stiff, glossy mixture.

4. Put the flour, cocoa powder, baking powder and salt in a large mixing bowl and mix together.

5. Add the oil, vanilla and melted chocolate to the dry ingredients and whisk until a smooth batter is formed.

6. Fold the aquafaba into the batter, a spoonful at a time, until fully incorporated and there are no specks of white visible.

7. Finally fold in the chocolate chunks until they are evenly distributed. Place the brownie batter into the lined tin and spread evenly.

8. Bake the brownie for 30 minutes, then leave to cool fully before slicing into nine squares. Enjoy!

vegan butter, for greasing

150g (5½oz) vegan dark chocolate, broken into pieces

100ml (3½fl oz) aquafaba (see page 149)

¼ tsp cream of tartar

150g (5½oz) caster (granulated) sugar

120g (4¼oz) plain (all-purpose) flour

40g (1½oz) cocoa powder

¾ tsp baking powder

½ tsp salt

80ml (2½fl oz) vegetable oil

1 tsp vanilla extract

100g (3½oz) vegan chocolate chunks

Makes 9

GLUTEN-FREE FRUIT AND NUT FLAPJACK

Bake it Simple If you aren't avoiding gluten, you can use normal flour and cornflakes.

There are hundreds of flapjack recipes available, but I am very particular about how I like mine. The addition of crushed cornflakes – to add an extra crunch – along with juicy fruit makes a winning combination.

1. Preheat the oven to 190°C (375°F) fan. Grease a 20cm (8 inch) square baking tin with butter and line with baking parchment.

2. Put the butter and golden syrup in a large saucepan over a medium heat. Stir until the butter has completely melted, then take off the heat.

3. Add the soft light brown sugar and stir until the butter and sugar have combined fully.

4. Add the oats, flour and crushed cornflakes to the pan and stir until combined. (You can mix everything in a mixing bowl if your pan isn't big enough.) Finally, add the chopped nuts and fruit and stir until they are evenly distributed.

5. Tip the mixture into the lined tin, then spread level and press it down. Bake for 15–20 minutes until golden brown. Leave to cool fully before cutting into nine squares. Enjoy!

200g (7oz) vegan butter, plus extra for greasing

50g (1¾oz) golden syrup (light corn syrup)

200g (7oz) soft light brown sugar

100g (3½oz) porridge oats

100g (3½oz) gluten-free self-raising flour

150g (5½oz) gluten-free cornflakes, crushed up

50g (1¾oz) nuts, roughly chopped (use whatever you fancy – I like to use pistachios)

100g (3½oz) dried fruit (I like to use cranberries)

Makes 9

PEANUT BUTTER MILLIONAIRE'S SHORTBREAD

Adding peanuts to a traditional millionaire's shortbread is game changing. The peanuts in the base add extra texture, whilst the smooth peanut butter makes the caramel even creamier.

1. Preheat the oven to 180°C (350°F) fan. Grease a 20cm (8 inch) square baking tin with butter and line with baking parchment, allowing some to overhang to help remove the shortbread from the tin later.

2. For the shortbread base, put the butter and sugar into the bowl of a stand mixer, if you have one – or into a large mixing bowl if you are using an electric hand whisk – and cream together until light in colour and fluffy. Add the vanilla and mix again until fully combined.

3. Place the peanuts in a sandwich bag and roughly crush with a rolling pin into smaller chunks, but don't grind them too finely.

4. Add the flour, salt and peanuts to the butter mixture and stir until fully combined and it resembles a clumpy and crumbly mixture.

5. Tip this into the tin and press down to create an even layer on the base of the tin. Use a fork to prick the base, then place in the fridge to chill for 10 minutes.

6. Bake the shortbread for 20–25 minutes until lightly golden in colour. Place the tin on a cooling rack to cool.

7. For the caramel, put the sugar, butter, condensed milk and peanut butter into a medium pan and place over a low–medium heat until the butter and sugar have completely melted.

8. Once fully combined, add the salt, then turn up the heat to medium–high and bring to a rapid boil. Boil for 5–8 minutes until it becomes darker in colour and much thicker – you should be able to see a line along the bottom of the pan when you drag a spoon through the caramel. Stir constantly to prevent the caramel from burning on the bottom of the pan. Remove from the heat and allow to stand until it has stopped boiling, then pour the caramel over the cooled base.

For the shortbread:
140g (5oz) vegan butter, plus extra for greasing

40g (1½oz) caster (granulated) sugar

1 tsp vanilla extract

50g (1¾oz) shelled peanuts

200g (7oz) plain (all-purpose) flour

a pinch of salt

For the caramel:
90g (3¼oz) caster (granulated) sugar

90g (3¼oz) vegan butter

1 x 370g (13oz) can of vegan condensed milk

50g (1¾oz) smooth natural peanut butter

½ tsp salt

50g (1¾oz) shelled peanuts

For the chocolate topping:
150g (5½oz) vegan dark chocolate

50g (1¾oz) vegan white chocolate

Makes 9

Continued overleaf...

9. Place the peanuts in the sandwich bag and crush roughly, then scatter evenly across the caramel. Push the peanuts into the caramel with a spoon to ensure they stick well. Place in the fridge to set for 30 minutes to an hour.

10. For the topping, put the dark chocolate and white chocolate into two separate bowls, then either melt in short bursts in the microwave or over a saucepan of gently simmering water.

11. Pour the dark chocolate over the top of the cooled caramel and level out. Spoon small dots of white chocolate onto the dark and use a cocktail stick to drag the white chocolate in various directions to create a feathered effect. Place back in the fridge until the chocolate is fully set – around an hour should be fine.

12. Use a hot knife to cut into nine squares, then allow to come back to room temperature to serve. Enjoy!

WHITE CHOCOLATE AND RASPBERRY BLONDIES

You can't go too far wrong with a good blondie. The addition of dark brown sugar gives them a richer, slightly molasses undertone that highlights the white chocolate chunks.

1. Preheat the oven to 180°C (350°F) fan. Grease a 20cm (8 inch) square baking tin with butter and line with baking parchment.

2. Melt the butter in a saucepan over low–medium heat. Once melted, transfer it to a large mixing bowl, add both the sugars and the vanilla extract, and mix until fully combined.

3. Add the flour, baking powder and salt, then mix until fully combined. Mix in the plant milk until you have a smooth batter. If you have a balloon whisk, it's good for getting out the lumps, but a wooden spoon is fine.

4. Chop 150g (5½oz) of the white chocolate into chunks, add them to the batter and mix until fully incorporated, setting aside the remaining chocolate for the top.

5. Finally, gently fold in most of the raspberries, reserving a few for the top, trying not to overmix so they don't break up too much.

6. Pour the batter into the lined tin and spread evenly, then scatter the last few raspberries over the top. Bake for 25 minutes if you prefer them more fudgy, or 30 minutes for a cakier texture. Once baked, remove from the oven and leave to cool in the tin on a wire rack.

7. Once cool, remove from the tin. Melt the remaining 50g (1¾oz) of white chocolate and drizzle over the top. Let the chocolate set, then cut into nine squares. Enjoy!

125g (4½oz) vegan butter, plus extra for greasing

120g (4¼oz) soft light brown sugar

80g (2¾oz) soft dark brown sugar (or use light brown)

1 tbsp vanilla extract

225g (8oz) plain (all-purpose) flour

¾ tsp baking powder

½ tsp salt

80ml (2½fl oz) plant milk (I use soya)

200g (7oz) vegan white chocolate

150g (5½oz) fresh or frozen raspberries

Makes 9

Bake it Simple These are so versatile! You can substitute the white chocolate and raspberries for your favourite flavours, such as dark chocolate and nuts.

FRUIT CRUMBLE SLICES

Bake it Simple Try serving these warm with custard for the perfect dessert.

One of my dad's favourite bakes are date slices, but I much prefer to use raspberries. The sourness of the soft fruit works perfectly with the crunchy oat topping. Feel free to use whatever fruit you like best – blackberries work really well too.

1. Preheat the oven to 180°C (350°F) fan. Grease a 20cm (8 inch) square baking tin with butter and line with baking parchment.

2. In a large bowl, rub the butter and flour together between your fingertips until the mixture resembles rough breadcrumbs. If you have a food processor, you can do this by pulsing the two ingredients together.

3. Add the oats and the sugar to the bowl and stir until fully combined.

4. Finally, add the plant milk and stir until the mixture starts to clump together in larger pieces.

5. Place half of the mixture into the base of the lined tin and press down with your fingers. Don't worry about it being exactly half – as long as the mixture covers the base of the tin with no gaps, it will work great.

6. Spread your chosen fruit evenly on top of the crumble base so you have a full layer of fruit.

7. Cover the fruit with the remaining crumble mixture, spreading it out to ensure there is an even layer on top. Finally, sprinkle over the almonds to add a nice crunch.

8. Gently press the crumble layer down with your hands, then bake for 30–35 minutes until lightly golden on top. Remove from the oven and leave to cool before slicing into eight slices. Enjoy!

150g (5½oz) vegan butter, plus extra for greasing

250g (9oz) self-raising flour

70g (2½oz) porridge oats

150g (5½oz) soft light brown sugar

50ml (1¾fl oz) plant milk

300g (10½oz) fresh or frozen raspberries, or berries of choice

30g (1oz) flaked (sliced) almonds

Makes 8

CHOCOLATE CHIP BROOKIES

Bake it Simple These brookies require a slightly longer bake than other recipes, but be patient as they are worth the wait.

Sometimes all you want in life is a cookie and a brownie at the same time. The chewy cookie base and soft fudgy brownie top are made for each other.

1. Preheat the oven to 160°C (315°F) fan. Grease a 20cm (8 inch) square brownie tin with butter and line with baking parchment.

2. For the cookie base, put the butter and both sugars into the bowl of a stand mixer, if you have one – or into a large mixing bowl if you are using an electric hand whisk – and beat together until light in colour and fluffy.

3. Add the salt, plant milk and vanilla and mix to combine. Add the flour and mix again until a smooth cookie dough forms. Finally, fold in the chocolate chunks. Tip the cookie dough into the lined tin and flatten down evenly to cover the base. Place in the freezer whilst making the brownie batter.

4. For the brownie layer, place the dark chocolate in a heatproof bowl and melt either in the microwave in 30 second increments, or over a pan of gently simmering water.

5. In a large bowl, mix together the flour, cocoa powder, salt and caster sugar. Add the oil, vanilla and plant milk to the dry ingredients and whisk until a smooth batter forms. Pour in the melted chocolate and thoroughly combine, then fold in the chocolate chunks.

6. Take the cookie dough out of the freezer and pour the brownie batter over the base. Level out with a spatula.

7. Bake for 45 minutes until you have a nice shiny top. Leave to cool for about 30 minutes until the tin is cool enough to touch. Then remove the brookies from the tin and place in the fridge to cool completely before slicing into nine squares. Enjoy!

For the cookie base:

120g (4¼oz) vegan butter, plus extra for greasing

100g (3½oz) soft light brown sugar

120g (4¼oz) caster (granulated) sugar

½ tsp salt

50ml (1¾fl oz) plant milk

1 tsp vanilla extract

220g (7¾oz) self-raising flour

150g (5½oz) vegan chocolate chunks

For the brownie top:

200g (7oz) vegan dark chocolate, broken into pieces

140g (5oz) plain (all-purpose) flour

40g (1½oz) cocoa powder

a pinch of salt

200g (7oz) caster (granulated) sugar

80ml (2½fl oz) vegetable oil

1 tsp vanilla extract

240ml (8fl oz) plant milk

75g (2½oz) vegan chocolate chunks

Makes 9

FONDANT
FANCIES

These are guaranteed to impress even the most critical of people. They are so much fun to make and are the perfect gift if you pop them in cupcake boxes and wrap with a bow.

1. Preheat the oven to 180°C (350°F) fan. Grease a 20cm (8 inch) square baking tin with butter and line with baking parchment.

2. Put the aquafaba and cream of tartar in the bowl of a stand mixer, if you have one – or into a large mixing bowl if you are using an electric hand whisk – and whisk on high speed with the balloon whisk attachment until it reaches stiff peaks. Set aside.

3. Meanwhile, put the soya milk in a jug and heat in the microwave for 1 minute to warm through (alternatively you can do this in a pan on the hob). Once warmed, mix in the apple cider vinegar and place to the side to curdle – this will take about 5 minutes.

4. In a large mixing bowl, combine the flour, sugar, bicarbonate of soda, baking powder, salt and lemon zest and mix until combined.

5. Once the soya milk has curdled, add the oil and vanilla to the same jug and mix thoroughly, then pour it into the dry ingredients. Whisk until a smooth batter is formed and there are no lumps of flour – try not to over mix. Finally, fold in the whipped aquafaba, one spoonful at a time, trying not to knock too much air out of the batter.

6. Pour the cake batter into the lined tin and bake for 40 minutes, or until a skewer inserted into the centre of the cake comes out clean. Leave on a cooling rack until the tin is cool enough to touch, then remove the cake from the tin and leave on the cooling rack to cool fully.

7. Whilst the cake is cooling, make the American buttercream using the ingredient quantities opposite and following the directions on page 171. Place the buttercream in the freezer so that you can roll it into balls later.

Continued overleaf...

For the sponge:
50ml (1¾fl oz) aquafaba (see page 149)

¼ tsp cream of tartar

290ml (10fl oz) soya milk

1 tbsp apple cider vinegar

300g (10½oz) plain (all-purpose) flour

275g (9¾oz) caster (granulated) sugar

1 tsp bicarbonate of soda (baking soda)

¼ tsp baking powder

½ tsp salt

zest of 1 lemon

140ml (4¾fl oz) vegetable oil

1 tbsp vanilla extract

For the American buttercream:
75g (2½oz) vegan butter, plus extra for greasing

150g (5½oz) icing (confectioners') sugar

a drop of plant milk, if needed

1 tsp vanilla extract

For the fondant icing:
1kg (2lb 4oz) fondant icing (confectioners') sugar

food colours (I use pink and yellow)

cocoa powder (optional)

Makes 16

8. For the fondant icing, divide the icing sugar into three bowls, setting a small amount aside to keep white for drizzling on top. Gradually add water to each bowl until it is a thick but pourable consistency. Add your chosen colour to each bowl – I use pink, yellow and a small amount of cocoa powder for brown.

9. Once the cake is completely cool, cut it into 16 squares. Remove the buttercream from the freezer, and scoop out a teaspoon for each fondant fancy and roll into a ball between your hands. Place a ball of buttercream onto each square of cake.

10. Place the cakes onto a cooling rack and put a tray underneath to catch the excess icing. Pour fondant icing over each cake until they are completely covered; some you may have to cover twice. Leave the icing to set.

11. Add a few drops of water to your reserved icing sugar to make a white icing. Put it into a piping bag and drizzle over the cakes to finish. Enjoy!

HONEYCOMB CHOCOLATE TIFFIN

Bake it Simple You can use whatever you have in your cupboards for this tiffin. Try using Biscoff biscuits instead of the honeycomb if you don't have any.

This tiffin is one of the simplest recipes, requiring no baking and minimal effort without any compromise on taste. The crunchy honeycomb pieces make a nice change from the biscuits you would usually expect to find!

1. Grease a 20cm (8 inch) square baking tin with butter and line with baking parchment, allowing some to overhang to help remove the tiffin from the tin later.

2. Put the butter, golden syrup and dark chocolate in a saucepan over a medium heat. Stir until the butter and chocolate have melted and the ingredients are fully combined.

3. Stir in the cocoa powder and salt until a smooth mix forms, then add the nuts, raisins and honeycomb and mix until they are evenly distributed and fully coated in the chocolate mixture.

4. Tip the mixture into the lined tin, spreading it evenly across the base. Place in the fridge for an hour to firm up.

5. Once the tiffin is firm, melt the remaining chocolate, either in the microwave for 30 second intervals or in a heatproof bowl set over a pan of simmering water. Pour the melted chocolate over the tiffin and spread evenly. Break up the remaining honeycomb into smaller pieces, then scatter over the melted chocolate.

6. Place back into the fridge to set for at least an hour, or until the chocolate is completely set. Cut into nine squares and enjoy!

150g (5½oz) vegan butter, plus extra for greasing

100g (3½oz) golden syrup (light corn syrup)

100g (3½oz) vegan dark chocolate, broken into pieces

30g (1oz) cocoa powder

a pinch of salt

75g (2½oz) pecans, roughly chopped (or any nut of choice)

75g (2½oz) raisins (or any dried fruit of choice)

75g (2½oz) honeycomb, roughly broken into small chunks

For the topping:
150g (5½oz) vegan dark chocolate, broken into pieces

20g (¾oz) honeycomb

Makes 9

BANOFFEE PIE SLICES

These slices have every component of a traditional banoffee pie but are so much easier to share around. They require slightly more effort than some of the other traybakes but are, without a doubt, worth it. Chewy caramel with a crunchy base, topped with softly whipped vegan cream – bliss!

1. Grease a 20cm (8 inch) square baking tin with butter and line with baking parchment.

2. For the biscuit base, place the digestives in a sandwich bag or something similar, and bash gently with a rolling pin to crush into a fine crumb, trying to remove all the big lumps of biscuit. Melt the butter, then add both the biscuit crumbs and the butter to a large bowl and mix thoroughly.

3. Tip the biscuit mixture into the lined tin and press down firmly to create an even layer across the base of the tin. Place in the freezer whilst making the filling.

4. For the caramel, put the sugar, butter and condensed milk into a saucepan and place over a low–medium heat until the butter and sugar have completely melted.

5. Once fully combined, add the salt and vanilla extract, then turn up the heat to medium–high and bring to a rapid boil. Boil for 5–8 minutes until it becomes darker in colour and much thicker – you should be able to see a line along the bottom of the pan when you drag a spoon through the caramel. Stir constantly to prevent the caramel from burning to the bottom of the pan. Remove from the heat and allow to stand until it has stopped boiling.

6. Once the caramel has stopped boiling, remove the base from the freezer and pour the caramel over, levelling out with a spatula to create an even layer.

7. Roughly slice the bananas and arrange them in a flat layer on top of the caramel. Place in the fridge to cool completely.

8. Whip the cream with the icing sugar until it forms stable peaks. Once the caramel is cool, cover with the cream, using the back of a spoon to spread it right to the edges. Decorate with chocolate shavings if desired before cutting into nine squares. Enjoy!

Bake it Simple If you like your caramel to be chewy, boil for closer to 8 minutes, but for softer set don't boil longer than 5 minutes.

For the base:
200g (7oz) digestive biscuits (graham crackers)

100g (3½oz) vegan butter, plus extra for greasing

For the caramel filling:
70g (2½oz) soft light brown sugar

70g (2½oz) vegan butter

1 x 370g (13oz) can of vegan condensed milk

½ tsp salt

1 tsp vanilla extract

For the topping:
2 large bananas

200ml (7fl oz) vegan double (heavy) cream (I recommend Oatly Whippable)

1 tbsp icing (confectioners') sugar

chocolate shavings (optional)

Makes 9

SCHOOL SPRINKLE CAKE

Bake it Simple You can switch up the flavours by adding a little orange or lemon zest to the cake batter and switching the water in the icing for fruit juice.

One of the most vivid memories of my school life was this simple vanilla iced traybake. This is the perfect addition to any party or bake sale, being extremely easy to make and a total crowd pleaser.

1. Preheat the oven to 160°C (315°F) fan. Grease a 30 x 23cm (12 x 9 inch) baking tin with butter and line with baking parchment.

2. Put the soya milk in a jug and heat in the microwave for 1 minute to warm through (alternatively you can do this in a pan on the hob). Once warmed, mix in the apple cider vinegar and place to the side to curdle – this will take about 5 minutes.

3. Put the butter and sugar into the bowl of a stand mixer, if you have one – or into a large mixing bowl if you are using an electric hand whisk – and cream together until light in colour and fluffy. Add the vanilla and mix again until fully combined.

4. Sift the flour into the butter and sugar, then add the curdled milk mixture and mix until all of the ingredients are fully combined and a smooth cake batter is formed.

5. Pour the batter into the lined tin and level out with a spatula. Bake for 50–55 minutes until golden brown and a skewer inserted into the centre of the cake comes out clean. Leave on a cooling rack until the tin is cool enough to touch, then gently remove the cake from the tin and leave to cool fully.

6. Put the icing sugar in a bowl and mix in enough water to give you a thick but pourable icing. Cover the cooled sheet cake with the icing, then generously cover with sprinkles to finish. Once the icing is set, cut into 12–15 squares depending on how large you want the slices to be. Enjoy!

For the sponge:

400ml (14fl oz) soya milk

2 tbsp apple cider vinegar

400g (14oz) vegan butter, plus extra for greasing

400g (14oz) caster (granulated) sugar

1 tbsp vanilla extract

400g (14oz) self-raising flour

For the icing:

450g (1lb) icing (confectioners') sugar

multicoloured sprinkles

Serves 12–15

Pastry

For the majority of the pastry recipes, I have used sweet shortcrust pastry. I really love my homemade recipe; perfect crispy pastry is guaranteed, every time. With that in mind, this book is aimed at reducing the faff, so feel free to use shop-bought shortcrust pastry – most are vegan (check the ingredients on the back) and do make the bakes even simpler. The key to working with pastry is to keep the vegan butter cold and try not to let the pastry get warm as it soon gets sticky and becomes difficult to work with. Make sure you flour your work surface and rolling pin when rolling out the pastry if you aren't using two sheets of baking parchment, otherwise you risk it sticking and tearing. If you don't have baking beans (pie weights), then rice or pulses work well too. Finally, if you don't have a loose-based tart tin, it might be worth investing in one as it reduces your risk of breaking the delicate pastry.

BAKEWELL TART

Bakewell tarts are such a well-loved teatime treat that there was no doubt I needed the perfect recipe for one. The crisp pastry and soft chewy frangipane match so well with the slightly sharp jam – they are a real favourite. I have included a recipe for the pastry here, but you could use shop-bought pastry, if you prefer.

1. For the pastry, put all the ingredients except the water in a food processor and pulse until it has a texture like breadcrumbs. Add the water and pulse until it starts to come together into a ball. Tip it out onto a work surface and bring it together into a smooth dough, kneading gently. Alternatively, if you don't have a food processor you can do this by hand. Combine the flour, icing sugar, salt and lemon zest in a large bowl, then rub in the butter between your fingertips until it forms rough breadcrumbs. Add the water and bring together into a ball. Knead until smooth.

2. Roll out the pastry on a flour-dusted surface – or between two sheets of baking parchment – until it is around 3mm (⅛ inch) thick. Lay the pastry over a 23cm (9 inch) tart tin, then carefully push the pastry into the sides allowing the excess to hang over the edges. Place the pastry case into the freezer to chill for 20 minutes. Meanwhile, preheat the oven to 180°C (350°F) fan.

3. Once chilled, remove from the freezer and place a sheet of baking parchment into the case. Fill with baking beans (pie weights) or rice and bake for 15 minutes. Remove from the oven and take out the beans and parchment, then return to the oven for a further 12 minutes until the edges are a light golden brown.

4. Place the tin on a cooling rack to cool until the pastry is just warm to the touch. Trim the excess pastry around the top edge with a serrated knife.

Continued overleaf…

For the sweet shortcrust pastry (optional):

200g (7oz) plain (all-purpose) flour, plus extra for dusting

30g (1oz) icing (confectioners') sugar

½ tsp salt

zest of 1 lemon

100g (3½oz) vegan butter

2 tbsp ice-cold water

For the frangipane:

110g (3¾oz) vegan butter

110g (3¾oz) caster (granulated) sugar

¾ tsp almond extract

75ml (2½fl oz) plant milk

1 tsp lemon juice

35g (1¼oz) plain (all-purpose) flour

150g (5½oz) ground almonds

1½ tsp baking powder

For filling and topping:

75g (2½oz) raspberry jam (see page 169 or shop-bought) or jam of preference

around 9 fresh or frozen raspberries

a handful of flaked (sliced) almonds

30g (1oz) icing (confectioners') sugar

Serves 8–10

Bake it Simple **Instead of making one large Bakewell, use the same recipe to make four small tarts.**

5. For the frangipane, put the butter, sugar and almond extract into a saucepan over a low heat and stir until just melted. Remove from the heat and add the milk and lemon juice, then set aside. Put the flour, ground almonds and baking powder in a large bowl and mix well. Pour the butter mixture into the dry ingredients and mix until smooth.

6. Cover the base of the pastry case with the jam, spreading it out evenly. Spoon the frangipane mixture over the jam and level with a spoon. Arrange the fresh raspberries across the top and scatter over the flaked almonds.

7. Bake the tart for 28–30 minutes until a skewer comes out clean and the top is golden brown. Once baked, remove from the oven and leave to cool on a cooling rack until cool enough to handle, before removing from the tart case from the tin to cool further.

8. In a small bowl, mix the icing sugar with a teaspoon of water until smooth, then drizzle over the Bakewell to finish. Enjoy!

LEMON MERINGUE PIE

This is another classic dessert that seems complex to perfect, but these simple steps result in soft pillowy meringue on top of a smooth but sharp lemony filling – what's not to love. Take it along to a dinner party and impress your guests!

1. For the pastry, put all the ingredients except the water in a food processor and pulse until it has a texture like breadcrumbs. Add the water and pulse until it starts to come together into a ball. Tip it out onto a work surface and bring it together into a smooth dough, kneading gently. Alternatively, if you don't have a food processor you can do this by hand. Combine the flour, icing sugar, salt and lemon zest in a large bowl, then rub in the butter between your fingertips until it forms rough breadcrumbs. Add the water and bring together into a ball. Knead until smooth.

2. Roll out the pastry on a flour-dusted surface – or between two sheets of baking parchment – until it is around 3mm (⅛ inch) thick. Lay the pastry over a 23cm (9 inch) tart tin, then carefully push the pastry into the sides allowing the excess to hang over the edges. Place the pastry case into the freezer to chill for 20 minutes. Meanwhile, preheat the oven to 180°C (350°F) fan.

3. Once chilled, remove from the freezer and place a sheet of baking parchment into the case. Fill with baking beans (pie weights) or rice and bake for 15 minutes. Remove from the oven and take out the beans and parchment, then return to the oven for a further 12–15 minutes until the edges are a light golden brown.

4. Place the tin on a cooling rack to cool until the pastry is just warm to the touch. Trim the excess pastry around the top edge with a serrated knife.

5. For the lemon filling, put the lemon juice and soya milk in a saucepan with 100ml (3½fl oz) water and set over a low–medium heat. Mix the sugar and cornflour together in a bowl, then add to the pan. Whisk the ingredients together over a medium heat, adding the

turmeric for the yellow colour. Whisk continuously until the mixture has thickened and large bubbles start to form. Take off the heat and whisk in the vegan butter until fully incorporated, then leave to cool slightly in the pan.

6. Once the pastry case is cool (still in the tart tin), pour in the lemon filling and level the top with a spatula. Leave to cool and set fully – place in the fridge once cool enough to do so.

7. For the meringue topping, put the aquafaba and cream of tartar into the bowl of a stand mixer, if you have one – or into a large mixing bowl if you are using an electric hand whisk – and whisk on high speed until it reaches stiff peaks. Meanwhile, put the sugar and agar agar into a saucepan with 25ml (1fl oz) water and set over a medium heat, swirling until the sugar and agar agar have dissolved and the liquid becomes clear. Increase the heat slightly and allow to boil until a sugar thermometer reads 116°C (240°F).

8. Once it reaches this temperature, slowly pour the sugar syrup into the aquafaba in a steady stream whilst still whisking. Keep whisking until the bowl no longer feels warm to the touch – this may take a while so be patient with it. Once ready, the mixture will be glossy and stiff.

9. Once the filling has set, take the pastry case out of the fridge. Spoon the meringue on top to cover the lemon filling and use an angled spatula or the back of a spoon to spread the meringue evenly and create small peaks. To finish, use a blowtorch (or grill – see tip) to brown the meringue. Enjoy!

For the sweet shortcrust pastry (you can use shop-bought pastry if preferred):
200g (7oz) plain (all-purpose) flour

30g (1oz) icing (confectioners') sugar

½ tsp salt

zest of 1 lemon

100g (3½oz) vegan butter

2 tbsp ice-cold water

For the lemon filling:
200ml (7fl oz) lemon juice (4–5 large lemons)

60ml (2fl oz) soya milk

200g (7oz) granulated sugar

30g (1oz) cornflour (cornstarch)

a pinch of turmeric powder

70g (2½oz) vegan butter

For the meringue:
100g (3½oz) aquafaba (see page 149)

¼ tsp cream of tartar

75g (1½oz) caster (superfine) sugar

½ tsp agar agar powder

Serves 8–10

VANILLA CUSTARD SLICES

Bake it Simple The pre-rolled puff pastry sheets that you buy in supermarkets are generally vegan, so if you want to save time, use them!

Custard slices are my friend's absolute favourite – she was one of the main reasons I decided to go vegan and we searched for a vegan version for ages with no success. Once I had perfected this recipe, we both sat and ate the whole lot. They are exactly how we remembered.

1. For the pastry, put the flour, salt and cubed butter into a food processor and pulse until it resembles breadcrumbs. Once it reaches this stage, add the water – start with 8 tablespoons but you will probably need all 10 – and pulse until it starts to come together into a ball. Tip it out onto a work surface and knead until it forms a ball. Alternatively, if you don't have a food processor you can do this by hand. Rub the butter into the flour and salt using your fingertips until it resembles breadcrumbs. Then add the water and bring it together into a smooth dough.

2. On a lightly floured work surface, roll out the pastry into a rectangle measuring roughly 15 x 30cm (6 x 12 inches). With a short side of the rectangle in front of you, grate half of the frozen butter over the bottom two thirds of the pastry, then fold the top third down over the middle and the bottom third up as if you were folding a letter.

3. Do a quarter turn with the pastry, then repeat step 2, rolling out the pastry again, grating over the remaining half of the frozen butter, and folding into thirds like a letter, then leave to rest in the fridge for 30 minutes.

4. After the 30 minutes, repeat step 2 again but without adding any more butter, then leave to rest for a further 30 minutes.

5. Meanwhile, preheat the oven to 180°C (350°F) fan and line two baking trays with baking parchment.

Continued overleaf...

For the rough puff pastry (you can use shop-bought puff pastry if preferred):
320g (11¼oz) plain (all-purpose) flour

½ tsp salt

70g (2½oz) vegan butter block, cold and cubed

8–10 tbsp ice-cold water

150g (5½oz) vegan butter block, frozen

For the vanilla custard:
320ml (11fl oz) soya milk

the thick part of 1 x 400g (14oz) can of coconut milk (75% coconut extract)

130g (4¾oz) caster (granulated) sugar

35g (1¼oz) cornflour (cornstarch)

1 tbsp vanilla extract

1 tbsp vanilla bean paste (if you have it, if not add more vanilla extract)

a pinch of turmeric powder

For the icing:
200g (7oz) icing (confectioners') sugar

pink and yellow food colouring gels

Makes 8

6. Once chilled, divide the pastry in half. Roll out each half to a 20cm (8 inch) square and place each square on a lined baking tray. Bake for 10–15 minutes until golden in colour and crispy. Once baked leave to cool for around 30 minutes on the baking trays, then move onto a cooling rack to cool completely. Don't worry if the pastry puffs up a lot; once it is cooled, simply press it down flat with a tray.

7. For the custard, put the soya milk into a saucepan, along with the thick part of the can of coconut milk. Place over a medium heat and stir until the coconut milk has melted and combined with the soya milk. In a small bowl stir together the sugar and cornflour, then add this to the pan. Use a whisk to stir the mixture until the sugar and cornflour have dissolved.

8. Add the vanilla extract and bean paste and turmeric to the pan and continue to stir. Turn up the heat slightly and whisk continuously until the mixture begins to thicken – large bubbles should start to form and the custard should look significantly thicker. Once it reaches this stage, take off the heat and pour into a jug to cool slightly.

9. To assemble, trim the two pieces of pastry so they will fit inside a 20cm (8 inch) square tin. Place one piece of pastry on the bottom of the tin, then pour over the custard and level out with an angled spatula. Place the second square of pastry on top of the custard, with the bottom facing upwards so it is completely flat on top. Place in the fridge to cool completely – the custard will set as it cools.

10. Mix the icing sugar with 2–3 tablespoons water until a smooth icing forms – it should be thick but still pourable. Spread the icing over the pastry until it is completely covered. Draw lines of pink and yellow food colouring across the icing, then use a skewer to drag the colouring through the icing, alternating between up and down directions to create a feathered effect. Leave the icing to set fully.

11. Once fully set, remove from the tin and slice into eight pieces. Enjoy!

CHOCOLATE ORANGE TART

Bake it Simple If you don't have orange chocolate don't worry! You can use whatever chocolate you have in the house.

This is a one of the quickest no-bake desserts I've ever made. It requires minimal ingredients yet tastes so rich in flavour, with a smooth, delicate texture. You can serve the leftover cream on the side, too.

1. To make the base, crush the biscuits to a fine crumb, either in a food processor or by placing the biscuits in a sandwich bag and crushing with a rolling pin. Once crushed, put them in a bowl, add the melted butter and mix until all of the biscuits are coated.

2. Tip the buttery crumbs into a 20cm (8 inch) tart tin and press down as firmly as possible to create a flat base and sides – you can use the back of a spoon to do this. Place in the freezer to firm up whilst you make the filling.

3. For the ganache, heat the cream, either in the microwave or in a pan over a low–medium heat, until steaming and slightly starting to bubble. Take off the heat and add the chocolate. Make sure all of the chocolate is covered in the hot cream, then leave to stand for 1 minute. Once it has been left to stand, stir until the chocolate melts fully and a glossy ganache is formed.

4. Remove the base from the freezer and pour in the ganache. Level the top with a spatula so it is completely flat. Segment the clementine and arrange the segments across the top. Leave in the fridge for at least an hour or until completely set. Enjoy!

For the base:
200g (7oz) digestive biscuits (graham crackers)

100g (3½oz) vegan butter, melted

For the filling:
150ml (5fl oz) vegan double (heavy) cream

200g (7oz) vegan orange chocolate, broken into pieces

1 clementine

Serves 8

JAM TARTS

Bake it Simple These are the perfect thing for using up leftover pastry – just make as many as your leftovers will allow you to roll.

Jam tarts are up there with my go-to buys from bakeries. Whilst they are nothing extravagant, they never let you down in flavour, particularly if you use a homemade jam. They can be personalized to your preference – use your favourite jams or curds.

1. Preheat the oven to 180°C (350°F) fan.

2. For the pastry, put all the ingredients except the water in a food processor and pulse until it has a texture like breadcrumbs. Add the water and pulse until it starts to come together into a ball. Tip it out onto a work surface and bring it together into a smooth dough, kneading gently. Alternatively, if you don't have a food processor you can do this by hand. Combine the flour, icing sugar, salt and lemon zest in a large bowl, then rub in the butter between your fingertips until it forms rough breadcrumbs. Add the water and bring together into a ball. Knead until smooth.

3. Roll out the pastry on a flour-dusted surface – or between two sheets of baking parchment – until it is around 3mm (⅛ inch) thick. Cut out 12 rounds using an 8cm (3¼ inch) fluted cutter, or a simple round one if that's all you have. You might have to gather up the excess and re-roll a couple of times to get 12 circles. Place the pastry rounds into a shallow 12-hole muffin or cupcake tray, gently pressing the pastry right into the holes.

4. Spoon 1–2 teaspoons of your chosen filling into each pastry case. Use any leftover pastry to lattice the top of some of the tarts, or cut out shapes to place on top if you like. Bake for 15–18 minutes until the pastry is golden brown and the filling has started to bubble slightly. Leave to cool fully before serving. Enjoy!

For the sweet shortcrust pastry (you can use shop-bought pastry if preferred):
200g (7oz) plain (all-purpose) flour

30g (1oz) icing (confectioners') sugar

½ tsp salt

zest of 1 lemon

100g (3½oz) vegan butter

2 tbsp ice-cold water

For the filling:
1–2 tsp of jam or curd of your choice for each tart (see pages 168, 169 and 170 for homemade versions)

Makes 12

FRANGIPANE MINCE PIES

Bake it Simple You can add extra fruit to your mincemeat filling – try chopped up dried apricots or dates for a chewy addition.

I tried frangipane mince pies for the first time not so long ago and now I can't look back! The chewy topping adds an extra texture to the mincemeat filling. You won't buy a shop-bought mince pie again.

1. For the pastry, put all the ingredients except the water in a food processor and pulse until it has a texture like breadcrumbs. Add the water and pulse until it starts to come together into a ball. Tip it out onto a work surface and bring it together into a smooth dough, kneading gently. Alternatively, if you don't have a food processor you can do this by hand. Combine the flour, icing sugar, salt and lemon zest in a large bowl, then rub in the butter between your fingertips until it forms rough breadcrumbs. Add the water and bring together into a ball. Knead until smooth.

2. Roll out the pastry on a flour-dusted surface – or between two sheets of baking parchment – until it is around 3mm (⅛ inch) thick. Cut out eight rounds using a 12cm (4½ inch) fluted cutter, or a simple round one if that's all you have. You might have to gather up the excess and re-roll a couple of times to get eight circles. Place the pastry rounds into a muffin tray, gently pressing the pastry right into the holes. Place the muffin tray into the freezer whilst you make the frangipane. Preheat the oven to 180°C (350°F) fan.

3. For the frangipane, put the butter, almond extract and sugar into a saucepan over a low heat until just melted. Remove from the heat and add the milk and the lemon juice, then set aside. Put the flour, baking powder and ground almonds in a large bowl and mix well. Pour the butter mixture into the dry ingredients and mix until smooth.

4. Take the muffin tray out of the freezer and spoon a heaped tablespoon of mincemeat into the bottom of each case, filling around halfway full. Top each mince pie with frangipane, spreading evenly across the top, then sprinkle each pie with flaked almonds. Bake for 25–30 minutes until golden brown.

5. Once baked, remove the tray from the oven and leave to cool for around 30 minutes or until cool enough to remove the pies from the muffin tray and place on a cooling rack to cool completely. Once cool, dust with icing sugar to serve. Enjoy!

For the sweet shortcrust pastry (or you can use shop-bought pastry, if preferred):
200g (7oz) plain (all-purpose) flour
30g (1oz) icing (confectioners') sugar
½ tsp salt
zest of 1 lemon
100g (3½oz) vegan butter
2 tbsp ice-cold water

For the frangipane filling:
55g (2oz) vegan butter
½ tsp almond extract
55g (2oz) caster (granulated) sugar
40ml (1¼fl oz) plant milk
1 tsp lemon juice
20g (¾oz) plain (all-purpose) flour
¾ tsp baking powder
75g (1½oz) ground almonds

For the filling:
1 jar of vegan-friendly mincemeat (I like Robertson's but any will work well)
a handful of flaked (sliced) almonds
1 tbsp icing (confectioners') sugar

Makes 8

BLUEBERRY BAKEWELL SLICES

Bake it Simple For an extra crunch, add some chopped up blanched almonds to the frangipane when you add the blueberries.

These slices are the perfect accompaniment to any picnic; you can cut them as large as you fancy depending on how many you're serving. The little bursts of fresh blueberry add an extra surprise to a traditional classic.

1. For the pastry, put all the ingredients except the water in a food processor and pulse until it has a texture like breadcrumbs. Add the water and pulse until it starts to come together into a ball. Tip it out onto a work surface and bring it together into a smooth dough, kneading gently. Alternatively, if you don't have a food processor you can do this by hand. Combine the flour, icing sugar, salt and lemon zest in a large bowl, then rub in the butter between your fingertips until it forms rough breadcrumbs. Add the water and bring together into a ball. Knead until smooth.

2. Roll out the pastry on a flour-dusted surface – or between two sheets of baking parchment – until it is around 3mm (⅛ inch) thick. Lay the pastry over a 30 x 20cm (12 x 8 inch) loose-based tart tin, then carefully push the pastry into the sides allowing the excess to hang over the edges. Place the pastry case into the freezer to chill for 20 minutes. Meanwhile, preheat the oven to 180°C (350°F) fan.

3. Once chilled, remove from the freezer and place a sheet of baking parchment into the case. Fill with baking beans (pie weights) or alternatively rice. Bake for 15 minutes. Remove from the oven and take out the beans and baking parchment then place back in the oven for a further 12 minutes until the edges are a light golden brown. Place the tin on a cooling rack to cool until the pastry is just warm to the touch. Trim the excess pastry around the top edge with a serrated knife.

4. For the frangipane, put the butter, sugar and almond extract into a saucepan over a low heat and stir until just melted. Remove from the heat and add the milk and lemon juice, then set aside. Put the

Continued overleaf...

For the sweet shortcrust pastry (or you can use shop-bought pastry if preferred):

200g (7oz) plain (all-purpose) flour

30g (1oz) icing (confectioners') sugar, plus extra for dusting

½ tsp salt

zest of 1 lemon

100g (3½oz) vegan butter

2 tbsp ice-cold water

For the filling:

150g (5½oz) blueberry jam (see page 168 or use shop-bought if preferred)

For the frangipane filling:

110g (3¾oz) vegan butter

110g (3¾oz) caster (granulated) sugar

¾ tsp almond extract

75ml (2½fl oz) plant milk

1 tsp lemon juice

35g (1¼oz) plain (all-purpose) flour

150g (5½oz) ground almonds

zest of 1 lemon

1½ tsp baking powder

150g (5½oz) fresh or frozen blueberries

Makes 12

flour, ground almonds, lemon zest and baking powder in a large bowl and mix well. Pour the butter mixture into the dry ingredients and mix until smooth. Gently fold three-quarters of the blueberries into the frangipane batter until they are evenly distributed, reserving the rest for the top.

5. Cover the base of the pastry case with the blueberry jam, spreading it out evenly. Spoon the frangipane mixture over the jam and level with a spoon. Arrange the remaining blueberries across the top.

6. Bake the tart for 28–30 minutes until a skewer comes out clean and the top is golden brown. Once baked, remove from the oven and leave to cool on a cooling rack until cool enough to handle, before removing from the tart case from the tin to cool further.

7. Once completely cool, dust with icing sugar and cut into 12 slices, or as many as you like depending on how big you'd like them to be. Enjoy!

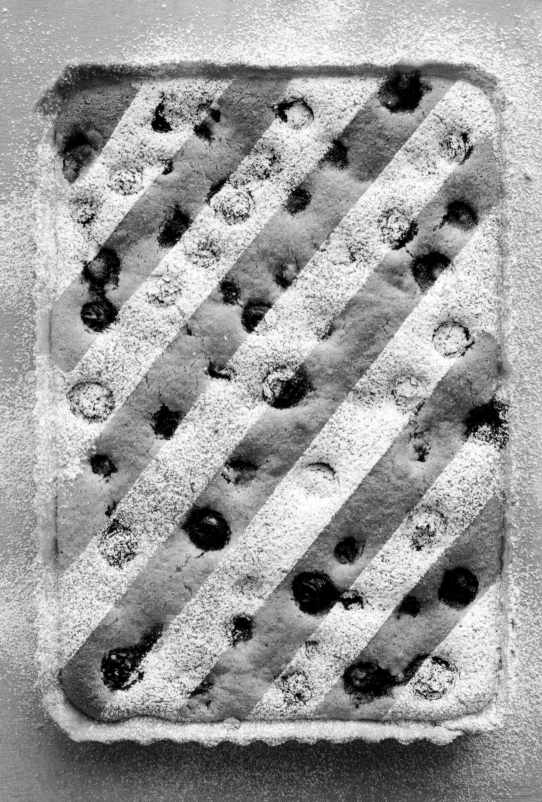

CUSTARD TARTS

Custard tarts are traditionally heavily egg based, but this creamy custard is full of vanilla flavour and completely plant based. These tarts make an impressive treat whilst being surprisingly easy!

1. For the pastry, put all the ingredients except the water in a food processor and pulse until it has a texture like breadcrumbs. Add the water and pulse until it starts to come together into a ball. Tip it out onto a work surface and bring it together into a smooth dough, kneading gently. Alternatively, if you don't have a food processor you can do this by hand. Combine the flour, ground almonds, icing sugar and salt in a large bowl, then rub in the butter between your fingertips until it forms rough breadcrumbs. Add the water and bring together into a ball. Knead until smooth.

2. Roll out the pastry on a flour-dusted surface – or between two sheets of baking parchment – until it is around 3mm (⅛ inch) thick. Cut out eight circles of pastry using a 12cm (4½ inch) fluted cutter, or a simple round one if that's all you have. You might have to gather up the excess and re-roll a couple of times to get eight circles. Place the pastry rounds into a muffin tray, gently pressing the pastry right into the holes. Place the muffin tray into the freezer whilst you make the custard. Preheat the oven to 180°C (350°F) fan.

3. For the custard, put the soya milk into a saucepan, along with the thick part of the can of coconut milk. Place over a medium heat and stir until the coconut milk has melted and combined with the soya milk. In a small bowl stir together the sugar and cornflour, then add this to the pan. Use a whisk to stir the mixture until the sugar and cornflour have dissolved.

4. Add the vanilla extract and bean paste and turmeric to the pan and continue to stir. Turn up the heat slightly and whisk continuously until the mixture begins to thicken. Once it has thickened slightly, take off the heat and pour into a jug.

5. Take the muffin tray out of the freezer and divide the custard between the pastry cases, filling each one almost to the top. If there is slightly too much custard for the cases don't worry – it tastes great eaten straight out of the jug! Sprinkle a pinch of nutmeg on top of each custard tart, then bake for 15–20 minutes. You should see the custard start to dome slightly, but take them out before it starts to bubble and boil over.

6. Once baked, allow to cool for around 30 minutes or until you are able to remove them from the tin to cool fully. Enjoy!

For the pastry:

150g (5½oz) plain (all-purpose) flour

50g (1¾oz) ground almonds

30g (1oz) icing (confectioners') sugar

½ tsp salt

100g (3½oz) vegan butter

2 tbsp ice-cold water

For the custard:

320ml (11fl oz) soya milk

the thick part of 1 x 400g (14oz) can of coconut milk (75% coconut extract)

130g (4¾oz) caster (granulated) sugar

35g (1¼oz) cornflour (cornstarch)

1 tbsp vanilla extract

1 tbsp vanilla bean paste (if you have it, if not add more vanilla extract)

a pinch of turmeric powder

a pinch of grated nutmeg for each tart

Makes 8

ECCLES CAKES

Eccles cakes are my mum's favourite thing to get from any bakery, so I had to include these just for her. The sugar on the outside of the flaky pastry caramelizes slightly in the oven, adding an extra crunch.

1. For the pastry, put the flour, salt and cubed butter into a food processor and pulse until it resembles breadcrumbs. Once it reaches this stage, add the water – start with 8 tablespoons but you will probably need all 10 – and pulse until it starts to come together into a ball. Tip it out onto a work surface and knead until it forms a ball. Alternatively, if you don't have a food processor you can do this by hand. Rub the butter into the flour and salt using your fingertips until it resembles breadcrumbs. Then add the water and bring it together into a smooth dough.

2. On a lightly floured work surface, roll out the pastry into a rectangle measuring roughly 15 x 30cm (6 x 12 inches). With a short side of the rectangle in front of you, grate half of the frozen butter over the bottom two thirds of the pastry, then fold the top third down over the middle and the bottom third up as if you were folding a letter.

3. Do a quarter turn with the pastry, then repeat step 2, rolling out the pastry again, grating over the remaining half of the frozen butter, and folding into thirds like a letter, then leave to rest in the fridge for 30 minutes.

4. After the 30 minutes, repeat step 2 again but without adding any more butter, then leave to rest for a further 30 minutes.

5. Meanwhile, preheat the oven to 200°C (400°F) fan and line a large baking tray or two smaller ones with baking parchment.

6. For the filling, put the butter and light brown sugar into a saucepan and set over a medium heat until the butter is fully melted. Take off the heat, add the spices and orange zest and juice and stir until fully combined. Finally stir in the currants until they are fully coated.

7. Once the pastry has finished resting, roll out until it is around 5mm (¼ inch) thick. Cut out six rounds using a 12cm (4½ inch) round cutter. Place a heaped tablespoon of the filling into the centre of each circle of pastry. Brush the edges of the circle with water, then gather up the pastry around the filling and pinch together. Flip over and flatten slightly, then place onto the lined baking tray, repeat with the remaining five pastry circles to make six Eccles cakes.

8. Brush the Eccles cakes with the milk, then sprinkle over the caster sugar. Make two small slits in the top of each cake, then bake for 15–20 minutes until they are light golden in colour. Once baked, place on a cooling rack to cool fully. Enjoy!

For the rough puff pastry:
320g (11¼oz) plain (all-purpose) flour

½ tsp salt

70g (2½oz) vegan butter, chilled and cubed

8–10 tbsp ice-cold water

150g (5½oz) vegan butter, frozen

For the filling:
70g (2½oz) vegan butter block

150g (5½oz) soft light brown sugar

1 tsp ground cinnamon

1 tsp ground ginger

1 tsp mixed spice (apple pie spice)

zest of 1 orange

1 tbsp orange juice

170g (6oz) currants

To assemble:
plant milk, for glazing

caster (granulated) sugar, for sprinkling

Makes 6

Desserts

A few of the recipes in this chapter, pavlova being one of them, use aquafaba – the liquid from a can of chickpeas (garbanzo beans). There are a few key tips to working with aquafaba, one being that the bowl and whisk must be completely clean and grease-free for it to whip up properly. To ensure this, I always get a little apple cider vinegar on a piece of kitchen paper and wipe it round the bowl and the whisk to remove any dirt. Secondly, some aquafaba is thicker than others. The ideal liquid is a thick, light brown colour, so if you have access to a slightly fancier brand, I would recommend you try that. You can also buy aquafaba that is pre-packaged, which I tend to buy if I'm making a pavlova as I know it is nice and thick. If you do find your aquafaba is too liquid, you can place it in a pan over a medium heat and reduce it down a little to remove some of the excess liquid – just make sure you let it cool again before using. Finally, cream of tartar really helps the aquafaba to whip to stiff peaks and is generally available in all supermarkets.

Bake it Simple **If you are preparing ahead, bake the meringue the night before you want to serve it and leave it in the oven switched off overnight to allow it to cool fully.**

RASPBERRY PAVLOVA

If you are looking for a showstopping dessert to impress anyone, particularly those who aren't quite convinced by vegan food yet, this is the perfect choice. It takes little effort as the majority of the time is spent baking the meringue and leaving it to cool. You can mix up the toppings as much as you like – it really is a dessert to please everyone!

1. Preheat the oven to 100°C (200°F) fan. Line a large baking tray with baking parchment. Draw around a medium-sized dinner plate on the parchment (or something similar) to create a circle roughly 23cm (9 inches) in diameter. Use a glass to draw a smaller circle in the centre of the larger one to create a wreath-like shape.

2. Use a piece of kitchen paper dampened with a small amount of apple cider vinegar or lemon juice to wipe around the bowl of a stand mixer, if you have one – or a large mixing bowl if you are using an electric hand whisk – to remove any grease.

3. Add the aquafaba and cream of tartar to the bowl and whisk, with a balloon attachment, on medium speed at first so it doesn't splash around, then on high speed until it reaches stiff peaks. This means you could turn the bowl upside down and the aquafaba wouldn't move. Once it reaches this stage, turn the mixer down to medium speed and add the sugar, one spoonful at a time, making sure each spoonful is fully incorporated before adding another. Once all of the sugar is incorporated, add the xanthan gum and whisk on high speed until the mixture looks glossy and sticky.

4. Spoon the meringue onto the baking parchment, keeping it within the lines you have drawn, and spread out to create the wreath shape. Use an angled spatula or the back of a spoon to create smooth strokes of meringue up the sides. Bake for 2 hours 30 minutes, then leave the oven door shut but turn the oven off. Leave the pavlova inside for several hours until it is completely cool.

5. For the coulis, put the raspberries and icing sugar into a food processor and blitz until very smooth. Sieve the mixture into a jug, removing all of the seeds. If you don't have a food processor you can mash the raspberries with a potato masher until smooth, then stir in the icing sugar before sieving until smooth.

6. Once the meringue is cool and you are ready to serve it, whip the cream and icing sugar together until it reaches soft peaks. Place dollops of it over the top of the meringue. Drizzle spoonfuls of the coulis over the cream, then arrange the fresh raspberries on top to finish. Add the toppings just before you are serving the pavlova as the cream will make the meringue soften over time. Enjoy!

For the meringue:
apple cider vinegar or lemon juice, for degreasing

150ml (5fl oz) aquafaba (see page 149)

½ tsp cream of tartar

150g (5½oz) caster (superfine) sugar

½ tsp xanthan gum

For the raspberry coulis:
150g (5½oz) fresh raspberries

1–2 heaped tbsp icing (confectioners') sugar

To assemble:
100ml (3½oz) vegan double (heavy) cream (I like Oatly Whippable)

25g (1oz) icing (confectioners') sugar

a handful of fresh raspberries

Serves 10–12

STICKY TOFFEE PUDDING

Bake it Simple If you have any leftover pudding, place it in a bowl in the microwave the next day – it tastes just as good reheated.

This recipe is heavily inspired by one of my favourite cooks, food writers and role models, Nigella Lawson. She was one of the main reasons I fell in love with food and cooking. I treasure her recipe books and love to make vegan versions of her most famous recipes, one being this sticky toffee pudding.

1. Preheat the oven to 160°C (315°F) fan. Grease a 23cm (9 inch) square tin, or something similar, with butter.

2. Put the chopped dates in a bowl and pour over the freshly boiled water. Add the bicarbonate of soda and mix, then leave them to soak for 30 minutes.

3. Meanwhile, pour the soya milk into a jug and heat in the microwave for 1 minute to warm through (alternatively you can do this in a pan on the hob). Once warmed, mix in the apple cider vinegar and place to the side to curdle – this will take about 5 minutes.

4. Put the butter and black treacle into the bowl of a stand mixer, if you have one – or into a large mixing bowl if you are using an electric hand whisk – and beat together until light in colour and creamy. Add the muscovado sugar and beat again until fully combined. Add the curdled soya milk, flour and baking powder and mix together until fully combined. Finally, use a fork to crush the dates slightly in the water, then pour the dates and their soaking liquid into the batter and mix until evenly distributed.

5. Pour the batter into the tin and bake for 30–35 minutes until a skewer inserted into the centre of the sponge comes out clean.

6. Meanwhile, make the toffee sauce. Put the butter, muscovado sugar and treacle into a medium saucepan and heat over a low heat until the butter has melted and all the ingredients are combined. Stir in the cream, turn up the heat and cook until it is bubbling and thickened, then take off the heat.

7. Once the sponge is baked, remove from the oven and prick it all over with a skewer. Pour around one-quarter of the toffee sauce over the sponge to cover, then leave to stand for around 20 minutes. Pour over the remaining toffee sauce and serve with vegan custard or cream. Enjoy!

For the sponge:
200g (7oz) pitted dates, roughly chopped

200ml (7fl oz) freshly boiled water

1 tsp bicarbonate of soda (baking soda)

100ml (3½fl oz) soya milk

1 tbsp apple cider vinegar

75g (2½oz) vegan butter, softened, plus extra for greasing

2 tbsp black treacle

50g (1¾oz) dark muscovado sugar

200g (7oz) plain (all-purpose) flour

2 tsp baking powder

vegan custard or cream, to serve

For the toffee sauce:
150g (5½oz) vegan butter

300g (10½oz) dark muscovado sugar

1 tbsp black treacle

200ml (7fl oz) vegan double (heavy) cream, at room temperature

Serves 9

CHOCOLATE ORANGE CHEESECAKE

Generally, people make a cheesecake with a digestive biscuit base, but you can in fact use any biscuit you like. I think the chocolatey flavour of the Bourbon biscuits elevates this cheesecake. The gentle orange flavour throughout gives the silky-smooth filling a little something extra.

1. Start with the base. Line a 20cm (8 inch) loose-based cake tin with a circle of baking parchment. Alternatively, if you don't have a loose-based tin, you can place two strips of baking parchment overhanging the cake tin for easy release.

2. Melt the butter in a small bowl in the microwave or in a saucepan over a low heat. Crush the biscuits to a fine crumb, either in the food processor or by putting them in a sandwich bag and bashing with a rolling pin, making sure there are no large lumps. Mix the melted butter with the crumbs until fully combined. Tip the mixture into the cake tin and press down until there is a flat, even layer of biscuit over the base. Place in the freezer whilst you make the filling.

3. Put the cream cheese into the bowl of a stand mixer, if you have one – or into a large mixing bowl if you are using an electric hand whisk – and whisk on medium–high speed until smooth and there are no lumps. Once smooth, pour in the cream and mix on low to start, then increase the speed and whisk until the mixture is light and fluffy but thick. Sift in the cocoa powder and icing sugar and mix until fully combined.

4. Melt the chocolate in a small bowl in the microwave in short bursts or in a heatproof bowl over a pan of simmering water. Once melted, pour the chocolate into the cheesecake mixture and mix until a smooth and thick mixture is formed.

5. Take the base out of the freezer, pour the cheesecake mixture over the base and smooth the top with a spatula. Place in the freezer for 3–4 hours to set, or alternatively overnight in the fridge.

6. To make the candied oranges, put the sugar in a saucepan with 200ml (7fl oz) water and set over a medium heat. Add the orange slices to the pan, bring the water to a boil, then lower the heat and simmer for 10–15 minutes until the slices look transparent. Remove from the pan and allow to dry out on a piece of baking parchment. Sprinkle the 2 tablespoons of sugar evenly over the slices.

7. To decorate the cheesecake, sift cocoa powder over the top to give a light covering, then arrange the candied orange slices across the top. Enjoy!

For the base:
100g (3½oz) vegan butter

200g (7oz) Bourbon biscuits (or other chocolate cream sandwich biscuits)

For the filling:
200g (7oz) vegan cream cheese

250ml (9fl oz) vegan double (heavy) cream

20g (¾oz) cocoa powder, plus extra for dusting the top

40g (1½oz) icing (confectioners') sugar

100g (3½oz) vegan orange chocolate (I like the Rhythm 108 dark cocoa orange bar)

For the candied oranges:
200g (7oz) granulated sugar, plus 2 tbsp for sprinkling

1 orange, thinly sliced

Serves 12

RED WINE PLUM UPSIDE-DOWN CAKE

This is the perfect dessert for a cold wintry day, to be eaten out of a bowl sat under a blanket. The red wine flavour is subtle but helps to give the cake a moist sticky texture, which works perfectly with the dash of cinnamon.

1. Preheat the oven to 160°C (315°F) fan. Grease a deep 20cm (8 inch) cake tin (preferably not one with a loose base) with butter and line with baking parchment.

2. Put the red wine and brown sugar in a saucepan over a low–medium heat and simmer until the sugar has dissolved and it looks syrupy (around 5–10 minutes is fine).

3. Put the soya milk in a jug and heat in the microwave for 1 minute to warm through (alternatively you can do this in a pan on the hob). Once warmed, mix in the apple cider vinegar and place to the side to curdle – this will take about 5 minutes.

4. Meanwhile, put the flour, sugar, cinnamon, bicarbonate of soda and salt into a large bowl and mix together with a balloon whisk.

5. Once the soya milk has curdled, add the oil to the same jug and whisk together. Pour the wet ingredients into the dry ingredients and whisk together until a smooth mixture forms – try not to over-mix.

6. Pour the red wine syrup into the bottom of the cake tin, then arrange the plum halves around the base of the cake tin, flesh side down, on top of the red wine syrup. Pour the cake batter into the tin covering the plums and bake for 50 minutes or until a skewer inserted into the centre of the cake comes out clean.

7. Allow to cool until the tin is not too hot to the touch, then turn out the cake onto a serving platter or cake stand – make sure to do it confidently in one quick motion. You can slide a sharp knife underneath and trim the bottom if it has domed slightly, so that the cake sits flat. Serve hot or warmed up with vegan cream or custard. Enjoy!

For the red wine syrup:

125ml (4fl oz) vegan red wine

50g (1¾oz) soft light brown sugar

For the cake:

vegan butter, for greasing

225ml (7¾fl oz) soya milk

1 tbsp apple cider vinegar

235g (8½oz) plain (all-purpose) flour (can be subbed for gluten-free flour)

210g (7½oz) soft light brown sugar

1 tsp ground cinnamon

1 tsp bicarbonate of soda (baking soda)

½ tsp salt

90ml (3fl oz) vegetable oil

7–10 plums (depending how big they are), halved and pitted

vegan cream or custard, to serve (optional)

Serves 6–8

CHOCOLATE MOUSSE CAKE

This dessert is very much one for the chocolate lovers. It has a rich, moist sponge with a light bubbly mousse topping. It is both indulgent and delicate, finished with perfectly sweet raspberries.

1. Preheat the oven to 180°C (350°F) fan. Grease a deep, 20cm (8 inch) loose-based cake tin with butter and line with baking parchment.

2. For the chocolate cake, pour the soya milk into a jug and heat in the microwave for 1 minute to warm through (alternatively you can do this in a pan on the hob). Once warmed, mix in the apple cider vinegar and place to the side to curdle – this will take about 5 minutes.

3. Meanwhile, sift the flour, sugar, bicarbonate of soda, cocoa powder and salt into a large bowl. Make a well in the middle of the dry ingredients.

4. Once the soya milk has curdled, add the vegetable oil and the vanilla extract to the same jug and mix. Add the wet mixture to the dry ingredients and combine using a balloon whisk until just combined – try not to over-whisk.

5. Pour the batter into the cake tin, then bake for 40 minutes, or until a skewer inserted into the centre of the cake comes out clean. Leave on a cooling rack in the tin until cool enough to touch before removing the cake from the tin to cool completely. Whilst the cake is cooling, wash the cake tin as it will be used later to assemble.

6. Once the cake is cool, trim the top off with a sharp knife so the cake is flat, then place the cake back into the cake tin.

7. For the mousse layer, melt the chocolate in the microwave in 30-second bursts or in a heatproof bowl over a pan of simmering water, then leave to cool to room temperature but still runny.

For the cake:

vegan butter, for greasing

225ml (7¾fl oz) soya milk

1 tbsp apple cider vinegar

195g (7oz) plain (all-purpose) flour

210g (7½oz) caster (granulated) sugar

1 tsp bicarbonate of soda (baking soda)

40g (1½oz) cocoa powder

½ tsp salt

90ml (3fl oz) vegetable oil

1 tsp vanilla extract

For the mousse:

100g (3½oz) vegan dark chocolate

150ml (5fl oz) aquafaba (see page 149)

¼ tsp cream of tartar

100g (3½oz) caster (superfine) sugar

To top:

20g (¾oz) cocoa powder

a handful of fresh raspberries

Serves 12

Continued overleaf...

Bake it Simple Use a small amount of cider vinegar or lemon juice to wipe the bowl before you whisk your aquafaba, removing any grease which might prevent it from whipping up properly.

8. Put the aquafaba and cream of tartar into the bowl of a stand mixer, if you have one – or into a large mixing bowl if you are using an electric hand whisk. Whisk on high speed until it reaches stiff peaks, meaning the aquafaba doesn't move when the bowl is tipped upside down.

9. Turn the mixer down to medium speed, then add the sugar, one spoonful at a time. Once it has all been added, mix on high speed for 2 minutes until fully combined and you have a stiff glossy mixture.

10. Add 1 tablespoon of the aquafaba to the melted chocolate and mix until smooth, then gently fold this chocolate mixture into the rest of the aquafaba until fully combined.

11. Pour the mousse into the cake tin on top of the cake, then smooth the top with a spatula. Depending on how deep your cake tin is, you might have slightly too much mousse, in which case just tip it into a bowl and eat as a dessert later! Place the cake in the fridge and leave to set for a minimum of 2 hours. When it's ready, the mousse shouldn't wobble, and it should look firm enough to cut through.

12. To finish, dust cocoa powder over the top then pile the fresh raspberries into the centre. Enjoy!

MINT CHOC CHIP ICE CREAM SANDWICHES

Mint choc chip is my all-time favourite ice cream flavour – and it is one that is not often made vegan. These sandwiches have an unbelievably simple homemade ice cream that is so creamy no one would know it's vegan. These are the perfect dessert to eat in the sun on a hot day.

1. For the ice cream, line the base of a brownie tin, roughly 27 x 18cm (10¾ x 7 inches), with baking parchment.

2. Pour the cream into the bowl of a stand mixer fitted with a balloon whisk, if you have one – or into a large mixing bowl if you are using an electric hand whisk – and whisk until the cream reaches stiff peaks. Once it is very thick, add the condensed milk and whisk again until fully combined.

3. Add the peppermint extract and whisk in, then taste and add more if you like a stronger mint flavour. Add the green food colour, if using, then whisk one final time until the mixture is a pale mint green colour.

4. Fold in the chocolate chips until evenly distributed, then pour the ice cream into the brownie tin. Place in the freezer to set for a minimum of 4 hours, but overnight is great.

5. For the cookies, preheat the oven to 180°C (350°F) fan. Line two baking trays with baking parchment.

6. Put the butter and sugar into the bowl of a stand mixer or into a large mixing bowl and cream together until light in colour and fluffy. Add the salt, vanilla and milk and mix again until fully combined.

7. Sift in the flour and cocoa powder and mix to form a rough cookie dough. Finally add the chocolate chunks and mix until evenly distributed.

8. Split the mixture into 12 portions (roughly 35–40g [1¼–1½oz] each) and roll into balls. Split the dough balls between the two baking trays. Bake for 15 minutes, then remove from the oven and place an 8cm (3¼ inch) cookie cutter over each cookie to encourage the edges inwards to make an even, circular cookie. If they have spread a lot, use the cutter to cut out the circle and discard the edges. Leave to cool on the tray.

9. Once the cookies are cool and the ice cream is set, use the same cookie cutter you used earlier for the cookies and place it into the ice cream, pulling the cutter out to remove a ring of ice cream. Place a cookie either side of the ice cream and remove the cutter to create the perfect ice cream sandwich. Repeat with the remaining ice cream to create six sandwiches. Enjoy!

For the ice cream:
400ml (14fl oz) vegan double (heavy) cream (I like Oatly Whippable)

1 x 370g (13oz) can of vegan condensed milk

1½ tsp peppermint extract, or to taste

green food colouring (optional)

200g (7oz) vegan dark chocolate chips

For the cookies:
90g (1¼oz) vegan butter

165g (5¾oz) caster (granulated) sugar

a pinch of salt

¾ tsp vanilla extract

40ml (1½fl oz) plant milk

150g (5½oz) self-raising flour

20g (¾oz) cocoa powder

55g (2oz) vegan dark chocolate chunks

Makes 6

Bake it Simple Because we are cutting rings of ice cream, there will be a small amount left over; put this into a tub in the freezer to eat on its own.

PINEAPPLE UPSIDE-DOWN CAKE

Bake it Simple If you can't find maraschino cherries, glacé cherries also work really well!

This perfectly sticky pudding has lightly caramelized pineapple rings jewelled with bright red cherries, giving it a retro feel. The cake is soft, moist and unbelievably moreish.

1. Preheat the oven to 170°C (325°F) fan. Grease a 15cm (6 inch) cake tin (don't use one with a loose base) with vegan butter.

2. Put the sugar and butter for the topping into a saucepan over a low–medium heat and heat until the butter is melted. Pour the melted butter and sugar into the cake tin and spread out across the bottom.

3. Put the pineapple rings onto a piece of kitchen paper and blot them to remove excess moisture. Arrange the pineapple rings across the bottom of the tin, allowing some of the pieces to go up the side of the tin. Place a cherry in the centre of each pineapple ring.

4. For the sponge, pour the soya milk into a jug and heat in the microwave for 1 minute to warm through (alternatively you can do this in a pan on the hob). Once warmed, mix in the apple cider vinegar and place to the side to curdle – this will take about 5 minutes.

5. Meanwhile, put the butter and sugar into the bowl of a stand mixer, if you have one – or into a large mixing bowl if you are using an electric hand whisk – and cream together until light in colour and fluffy. Add the vanilla extract and mix until fully combined, then pour in the curdled milk, followed by the flour and baking powder. Mix until all the ingredients are combined and a smooth batter is formed.

6. Pour the batter into the cake tin on top of the pineapple rings and level the top with a spatula. Bake for 45–50 minutes until a skewer inserted into the centre of the cake comes out clean. It will still look very moist but that's fine as long as the skewer is clean.

7. Once baked, leave the cake to cool in the tin for 30 minutes, before turning out onto a plate. Do this by placing the plate on top of the cake tin, then flip over in one confident motion. You might have to tap the bottom of the tin to encourage the cake out. Enjoy!

For the pineapple topping:

60g (2oz) vegan butter, plus extra for greasing

45g (1½oz) soft light brown sugar

6–7 pineapple rings (a 425g [15oz] can of pineapple rings in juice)

6–7 maraschino cherries

For the sponge:

180ml (6fl oz) soya milk

1 tbsp apple cider vinegar

180g (6¼oz) vegan butter

180g (6¼oz) caster (granulated) sugar

1 tbsp vanilla extract

180g (6¼oz) self-raising flour

1 tsp baking powder

Serves 6–8

TIRAMISU

This is a simple version of a classic Italian dessert, but with all the key flavours and textures. The silky-smooth filling sits on top of softened homemade lady fingers, however you can also use shop-bought vegan ones for an even easier dessert. This tastes even better the next day when it has been kept in the fridge overnight.

1. Preheat the oven to 180°C (350°F) fan. Line two baking trays with baking parchment – you might need a third baking tray lined, depending on how large your lady fingers are.

2. Put the aquafaba and cream of tartar into the bowl of a stand mixer, if you have one – or into a large mixing bowl if you are using an electric hand whisk – making sure the bowl and whisk are very clean and have no grease on them. Whisk on high speed until the mixture reaches stiff peaks, then add the sugar, one spoonful at a time. Once fully incorporated, whisk on high speed for 2 minutes until glossy and stiff.

3. In a small bowl, whisk together the yogurt, oil and vanilla until combined. Fold this mixture into the aquafaba one spoonful at a time until fully incorporated. Sift the flour and baking powder into the bowl, then very gently fold it in until fully combined, trying to knock as little air out as possible.

4. Spoon the mixture into a piping bag fitted with a 1cm (½ inch) round nozzle. Pipe lines of the mixture, each around 7cm (2¾ inch) long, leaving a gap between each one to allow them room to spread. This will make between 30 and 40 fingers. Bake for 15–20 minutes until lightly golden on the edges. Once baked, leave to cool on the trays.

5. For the cream filling, whip the cream and icing sugar together until it is very thick and holds stiff peaks. Add the cream cheese and Tia Maria, then whip again until fully combined and you have a smooth cream. Spoon this into a piping bag fitted with a large round nozzle.

6. For the coffee soak, mix the Tia Maria into the coffee, then pour this into a shallow dish. Once the lady fingers are cool, dip them into the coffee mixture, flipping them over so they are fully covered. They want to soak up the coffee mixture, but not become soggy. Dip half of the lady fingers, then arrange them in an even layer in the base of a 20cm (8 inch) square dish or cake tin. Pipe a layer of the cream over the lady fingers so they are completely covered, then dust cocoa powder over the cream. Repeat with the remaining lady fingers, dipping them in coffee, then placing on top of the cream.

7. Pipe the remaining cream in small blobs across the top, then finish with a last dusting of cocoa powder. Enjoy!

For the lady fingers:
180ml (6fl oz) aquafaba (see page 149)

¼ tsp cream of tartar

170g (6oz) caster (superfine) sugar

80g (2¾oz) plain vegan yogurt

60ml (2fl oz) vegetable oil

2 tsp vanilla extract

310g (11oz) self-raising flour

½ tsp baking powder

For the cream filling:
250ml (9fl oz) vegan double (heavy) cream (I like Oatly Whippable)

100g (3½oz) icing (confectioners') sugar

170g (6oz) vegan cream cheese

1–2 tsp Tia Maria or other coffee liqueur

To assemble:
1 tbsp Tia Maria or other coffee liqueur

200ml (7fl oz) freshly brewed strong coffee

cocoa powder, for dusting

Serves 9

Bake it Simple If you don't have fresh coffee, you can use 200ml (7fl oz) of boiling water and 2 tbsp of instant coffee.

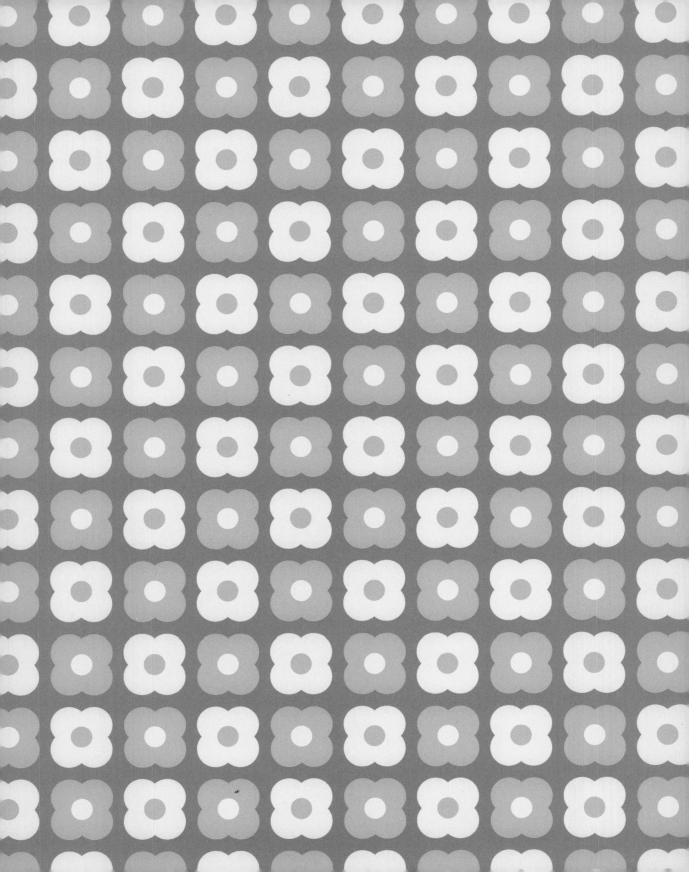

Extras

These jam recipes don't use a jam thermometer, as I find that if I use one, the jam runs the risk of boiling over and becoming too thick. The best way to ensure you make perfect jam is not to over-boil it. Place a saucer in the freezer for half an hour before you make the jam, then once the jam has boiled for a few minutes and looks darker and a little thicker, place a drop onto the cold saucer. If it wrinkles when you run your finger through, it is ready; remember the jam thickens as it cools. For the buttercreams, always make sure you use a vegan butter block rather than the spreadable kind otherwise your buttercream will be too soft and the wrong consistency. If you are making a simple American buttercream, just buy the supermarket own-brand 'baking block' which is generally and accidentally vegan (check the ingredients) – it is very cheap and works perfectly. For the more elaborate buttercreams like Italian or Swiss meringue and Russian buttercream, I find the more expensive vegan butter blocks work better; they are less likely to cause curdling and they create a smooth finish.

BLUEBERRY JAM

Blueberries have a unique flavour and are generally much sweeter than other berries. This jam is great if you fancy adding something a little different from the expected raspberry or strawberry jam. It also has the prettiest purple colour.

150g (5½oz) blueberries (fresh or frozen)

120g (4¼oz) jam sugar

juice of ½ lemon

Makes 1 small jar

1. Put the blueberries, jam sugar and lemon juice into a saucepan over a medium heat. Use a potato masher or a fork to crush the blueberries as they cook, but don't boil the jam at this point. Once the blueberries have been crushed, place a sieve over a jug, then pour the blueberry mixture into the sieve, pressing it through to remove all of the blueberry skin.

2. Pour the sieved liquid back into the pan, then place back over a medium heat and bring to the boil. As soon as it starts to bubble, allow to rapidly boil for around 3 minutes, stirring occasionally, then remove from the heat. You will be able to tell it's ready when it looks thicker, and the jam at the sides of the pan looks like it is sticking. You can test whether your jam is ready by placing a drop of it onto a cold plate – leave it for 1 minute, then if it wrinkles when you push your finger through the jam, it is ready.

3. Pour the jam into a sterilized jar, if you are using later, or into a bowl to cool if you are using for a recipe the same day. Enjoy!

CHERRY JAM

I like to keep the cherries in the jam without sieving them, as I think they add an extra texture, especially when you are using the jam for something like a Black Forest gateau. This is super quick and foolproof, and you don't need any fancy equipment like a jam thermometer.

250g (9oz) frozen pitted cherries

125g (4½oz) jam sugar

juice of 1 lemon

Makes 1 small jar

1. Put the cherries, jam sugar and lemon juice into a saucepan over a medium heat. As they cook, use a fork or a potato masher to crush the cherries until they are very soft.

2. Once the cherries are broken down into a chunky purée and it has started to bubble, allow to rapidly boil for 3–5 minutes, stirring occasionally, then remove from the heat. You will be able to tell it's ready when it looks thicker, and the jam at the sides of the pan looks like it is sticking. You can test whether your jam is ready by placing a drop of it onto a cold plate – leave it for 1 minute, then if it wrinkles when you push your finger through the jam, it is ready.

3. Pour the jam into a sterilized jar if you are using later, or into a bowl to cool if you are using for a recipe the same day. Enjoy!

RASPBERRY JAM

I like to use smooth seedless jam for my raspberry recipes – whilst there is nothing wrong with bits, in things such as a Swiss roll I find the smoother texture works much better. This has the perfect amount of sharpness to balance the sweetness of the fruit, and it is definitely better than shop-bought jam!

1. Put the raspberries, jam sugar and lemon juice into a saucepan over a medium heat. Use a potato masher or a fork to crush the raspberries until they are a pulp and there are no lumps; don't boil the jam at this point. Once the raspberries have been crushed, place a sieve over a jug and pour the mixture into the sieve, pressing it through to remove all of the seeds.

2. Pour the sieved liquid back into the pan, then place back over a medium heat and bring to the boil. As soon as it starts to bubble, allow to rapidly boil for 3–5 minutes, stirring occasionally, then remove from the heat. You will be able to tell it's ready when it looks thicker, and the jam at the sides of the pan looks like it is sticking. You can test whether your jam is ready by placing a drop of it onto a cold plate – leave it for 1 minute, then if it wrinkles when you push your finger through the jam, it is ready.

3. Pour the jam into a sterilized jar if you are using later, or into a bowl to cool if you are using for a recipe the same day. Enjoy!

100g (3½oz) fresh or frozen raspberries

80g (2¾oz) jam sugar

juice of ½ lemon

Makes 1 small jar

CRÈME PÂTISSIÈRE

This is basically fancy custard, perfect for filling things such as brioche buns or cakes. Once it has cooled, it will be thick enough to pipe. You can use this to make a crème diplomate by whisking together equal amounts of crème pâtissière and vegan double (heavy) cream.

1. Pour the soya milk into a saucepan and add the thick part of the can of coconut milk. Place over a medium heat and stir until the coconut milk has melted and combined with the soya milk.

2. In a small bowl, stir together the sugar and cornflour, then add this to the pan. Use a whisk to stir the mixture until the sugar and cornflour have dissolved.

3. Add the vanilla extract and bean paste and the turmeric to the pan and continue to stir. Turn up the heat slightly and whisk continuously until the mixture begins to thicken. Once it has thickened, take off the heat and pour into a bowl to cool. If you want thick crème pâtissière to pipe, keep on the heat slightly longer, or for a softer set custard, take it off when it starts to look thick. Cover with a damp piece of scrunched up baking parchment to stop it forming a skin. If it still forms a skin, don't worry – just give it a whisk until smooth. Enjoy!

320ml (11fl oz) soya milk

the thick part of 1 x 400g (14oz) can of coconut milk (75% coconut extract)

130g (4¾oz) caster (superfine) sugar

35g (1¼oz) cornflour (cornstarch)

1 tbsp vanilla extract

1 tbsp vanilla bean paste (if you have it – if not add more vanilla extract)

a pinch of turmeric powder

Makes enough to fill 1 cake

LEMON CURD

Where I live it is difficult to find vegan lemon curd in the supermarket, but this recipe is so quick and easy that I'm never disappointed. It works perfectly in so many recipes, like Viennese whirls or cupcakes, but my family also love to eat it on toast for breakfast.

1. Put the lemon juice and soya milk in a pan with 50ml (1¾fl oz) water and set over a low–medium heat. Mix the sugar and cornflour together in a bowl, then add to the pan. Continually whisk the ingredients in the pan over a medium heat, adding the turmeric for the yellow colour.

2. Whisk until the mixture starts to thicken and it coats the back of a spoon – it will set more as it cools so it still wants to be pourable. Take the pan off the heat and whisk in the vegan butter until fully incorporated.

3. Pour the curd into a sterilized jar if you are using later, or into a bowl to cool if you are using for a recipe the same day. Once cooled, keep the curd in the fridge if you aren't using it straight away. Enjoy!

100ml (3½fl oz) lemon juice (about 2 large lemons)

30ml (1fl oz) soya milk

100g (3½oz) granulated sugar

15g (½oz) cornflour (cornstarch)

a pinch of turmeric powder

35g (1¼oz) vegan butter

Makes 1 jar

PASSION FRUIT CURD

I often forget passion fruits exist, but they work so well in baking. This curd is a great addition to citrussy desserts and makes a change from traditional lemon curd. I sieve all the seeds from the curd, but feel free to leave some in if you like them.

1. Scrape out the seeds from the passion fruits into a saucepan and add the sugar, lemon juice and milk. Place over a low–medium heat and stir until the sugar has dissolved.

2. Once dissolved, pour the mixture through a sieve into a jug to remove the seeds then transfer the mixture back to the pan.

3. In a separate bowl, whisk together 3 tablespoons water and the cornflour until smooth, then add this to the passion fruit mixture. Whisk over a medium heat until it starts to thicken and coats the back of a spoon – it will set more as it cools so it still wants to be pourable.

4. Remove from the heat and whisk in the turmeric and butter until smooth.

5. Pour the curd into a sterilized jar if you are using later, or into a bowl to cool if you are using for a recipe the same day. Enjoy!

5 fresh passion fruits

200g (7oz) granulated sugar

juice of 1 lemon

110ml (3¾fl oz) soya milk

4 tbsp cornflour (cornstarch)

a pinch of turmeric powder

1½ tbsp vegan butter

Makes 1 jar

CHOCOLATE GANACHE

This chocolate ganache is so versatile – you can use it to create drips on a celebration cake, or alternatively leave it to cool and set, then roll it into balls for chocolate truffles. If you let it set until firm, then use an electric whisk to whip it up, you'll have a fluffy ganache that's perfect for filling cakes. Any vegan pouring cream will work; I like to use Elmlea plant double (heavy) cream.

75ml (2½fl oz) vegan pouring cream

100g (3½oz) vegan dark chocolate, broken into pieces

Makes enough to fill and top 1 cake

1. Heat the cream either in a bowl in the microwave or in a saucepan on the hob until it is steaming and small bubbles form around the edge.

2. Put the chocolate in a heatproof bowl and once the cream is hot, pour it over the chocolate, making sure all of the chocolate is submerged in the cream. Leave to stand for 1 minute.

3. Stir until the cream and the chocolate are combined and you have a smooth glossy ganache. Enjoy!

AMERICAN BUTTERCREAM

American buttercream is the most standard buttercream used for cakes. It is extremely easy to make with just two main ingredients, and is a simple way to fill and ice your celebration cakes. It is also the best icing to use if you are wanting to pipe flower decorations – just pop it in the fridge for 10 minutes beforehand. If you'd like to make chocolate buttercream, just switch out 30g (1oz) of icing sugar for the same amount of cocoa powder.

250g (9oz) vegan butter block

500g (1lb 2oz) icing (confectioners') sugar

1 tbsp plant milk

1 tbsp vanilla extract

Makes enough to fill and top 1 cake

1. Cut the vegan block into cubes, then place it into the bowl of a stand mixer fitted with a paddle attachment if you have one – or into a large mixing bowl if you are using an electric hand whisk. Mix on high speed until the butter looks creamy.

2. Add the icing sugar, milk and vanilla extract and mix with a wooden spoon until the icing sugar is combined slightly with the butter (this just stops the icing sugar going everywhere), then use the machine or electric whisk again to beat on high until fully combined.

3. Continue to beat the icing for another few minutes until it looks very soft and light – the longer you beat it, the fluffier it becomes, meaning it is a much nicer texture to eat. At this point you can add in any other flavours you want to. Enjoy!

ITALIAN MERINGUE BUTTERCREAM

This is my favourite type of buttercream to make for a special occasion. It takes a little extra effort but it results in a perfectly sweet and glossy buttercream that will elevate any cake.

1. Put the aquafaba and cream of tartar into the bowl of a stand mixer fitted with a balloon whisk if you have one – if not, use a large mixing bowl and an electric hand whisk. Whisk on high speed until the mixture reaches stiff peaks.

2. Meanwhile, put the sugar and 90ml (3fl oz) water in a saucepan over medium–high heat. Heat until the sugar dissolves and the syrup reaches 116°C (240°F) on a thermometer. Once it reaches this temperature, turn the mixer speed down to medium and slowly pour the syrup into the aquafaba. Once the syrup is added, increase the speed to high and continue to mix until the bowl feels cool.

3. Once cool, add the vanilla whilst still mixing, then slowly add the butter and shortening, one small cube at a time. The buttercream will look like it is deflating as you add the butter, but don't worry this is normal. Once all of the butter and shortening has been added, mix on high until silky smooth. Enjoy!

180ml (6fl oz) aquafaba (see page 149)

¼ tsp cream of tartar

200g (7oz) granulated sugar

170g (6oz) good-quality vegan butter block (I like Natrali or Flora Plant), diced and softened

85g (3oz) vegetable shortening (such as Trex), diced and softened

1 tbsp vanilla extract

Makes enough to fill and top 1 cake

SWISS MERINGUE BUTTERCREAM

This is slightly a cheat's version of Swiss meringue buttercream as it traditionally uses a bain marie. I have tested so many different methods and I find this one creates the perfectly light, silky smooth and slightly less sweet buttercream that everyone aims for with Swiss meringue, but without the extra hassle. This is the perfect filling for a celebration cake.

1. Cut the butter block into cubes, then place them into the bowl of a stand mixer fitted with a balloon attachment if you have one – or into a large mixing bowl if you are using an electric hand whisk. Whisk on high speed for a few minutes until the butter is light in colour and looks creamy.

2. Add the icing sugar and vanilla, then whisk again until fully incorporated and you have a light fluffy buttercream.

3. Pour in the aquafaba, then whisk again for around 5 minutes until it is completely smooth and glossy. Enjoy!

250g (9oz) good-quality vegan butter block (I like Natrali or Flora Plant), softened

325g (11½oz) icing (confectioners') sugar

1 tbsp vanilla extract

80ml (2½fl oz) aquafaba (see page 149)

Makes enough to fill and top 1 cake

INDEX

ACKNOWLEDGEMENTS

I'd like to say a huge thank you to the incredible team of people that helped make this book happen; I feel so grateful for each and every person that played a part in this process. Firstly, my agent Vivienne Clore who made this possible – it goes without saying how fabulous she is. I still can't thank Clare Winfield enough for how unbelievably perfect the photography turned out – every single picture is better than I ever imagined, she is so talented. JoJo Jackson, a brilliant food stylist, not only cuts the perfect slice of cake for each shot, but also makes the best frothy coffee. I am beyond grateful to Céline Hughes, my publisher, and Nikki Ellis, the designer, for helping make the vision I had for this book come to life. They have been my right hand (or left in my case) throughout this whole process and have helped me produce something I am so proud of. The beautiful props were styled by Hannah Wilkinson and really made each picture come to life.

My family have helped make this possible, not only by being supportive throughout, but for helping clear up the mess every day for months. Both family and friends have also eaten copious amounts of cake whilst I tested each recipe numerous times; without them I'd have been eating it all myself! Special thank you to Maggie, now a close friend, for testing lots of recipes for me – it was a huge help and very reassuring throughout the whole process.

Last but certainly not least, I have the incredible **Great British Bake Off** team to thank for giving me the platform for opportunities like **Simply Vegan Baking**. The experience was once in a lifetime, and allowed me to meet some of the most important people in my life.